Envision It! | Handbook

Grade 5

PEARSON

Glenview, Illinois • Boston, Massachusetts
Chandler, Arizona • Upper Saddle River, New Jersey

ISBN-13: 978-0-328-58088-0
ISBN-10:   0-328-58088-0
9 10 V056 18 17 16 15 14

CC1

Envision It! | Handbook

A note to you!

The *Envision It! Handbook* will help you learn more about comprehension strategies, comprehension skills, vocabulary, and genres. You can use it on your own, with a partner, or with your teacher. Take a look inside and you will find lessons, illustrations, photographs, and charts that will help you become a better reader!

A note to your teacher. . .

The *Envision It! Handbook* will help your students learn more about comprehension strategies, comprehension skills, vocabulary, and genres. You can use it in small groups to enhance your reading instruction, or students can use it on their own or with a partner to guide their reading.

The *Envision It! Handbook* is filled with lessons, illustrations, photographs, and charts that will help your students become better readers!

Envision It! | Handbook

Contents

Let's Think About Vocabulary

Let's Think About Genre

Envision It! | Visual Strategies

Background Knowledge

Important Ideas

Inferring

Monitor and Clarify

Predict and Set Purpose

Questioning

Story Structure

Summarize

Text Structure

Visualize

Comprehension Strategies

As you read,
• try to make sense of what you are reading by thinking about what you know.
• notice when you don't understand something.

Comprehension strategies are ways to think about reading in order to better understand what you read.

Ready to **Try** It? ▶

Background Knowledge

Background knowledge is what you already know about a topic based on your reading and personal experience. Make connections to people, places, and things from the real world. Use background knowledge before, during, and after reading to monitor comprehension.

To use background knowledge

- with fiction, preview the title, author's name, and illustrations
- with nonfiction, preview chapter titles, headings, captions, and other text features
- think about your own experiences while you read

That reminds me of the time we went to the basement during the tornado warning.

Let's Think About Reading!

When I use background knowledge, I ask myself

- Does this character remind me of someone?
- How is this story or text similar to others I have read?
- What else do I know about this topic from what I've read or seen?

Background Knowledge
The Skunk Ladder
by Patrick F. McManus

Background knowledge helps me make connections between my reading and what I already know. I think about:

What I know from my own life (text-to-self =).

What I know from the world (text-to-world = 🌎).

What I know from other things I've read (text-to-text = 📘).

Here are some connections I made while reading The Skunk Ladder.

In the summer, my friend Jeff and I sit around trying to think of something to do, like Eddie and the narrator.

When the skunk gets stuck in the hole, I thought about how my dad once trapped a raccoon in the garage by accident. The raccoon ran out the next time my dad opened the door!

I thought of Karana in Island of the Blue Dolphins because she is a problem solver, like Eddie and the narrator.

The setting reminds me of farms in Iowa or Kansas.

Important Ideas

Important ideas are essential ideas in a nonfiction selection. Important ideas include information and facts that provide clues to the author's purpose.

To identify important ideas
- read all titles, headings, and captions
- look for words in italics, boldface print, or bulleted lists
- look for signal words and phrases: *for example, most important,* and others
- use photographs, illustrations, or other graphic sources
- note how the text is organized—cause and effect, problem and solution, question and answer, or other ways

This must be an important idea.

Let's Think About Reading!

When I identify important ideas, I ask myself
- What information is included in bold, italics, or other special lettering?
- What details support important ideas?
- Are there signal words and phrases?
- What do illustrations, photos, diagrams, and charts show?
- How is the text organized?
- Why did the author write this?

Important Ideas
The Truth About Austin's Amazing Bats
by Ron Fridell

As I read The Truth About Austin's Amazing Bats, I looked for important ideas that would tell me why these bats are so amazing.

Important Ideas

1. Small, dark areas under the bridge are a perfect bat habitat.
2. In the summer, Austin has more bats than people!
3. Bat Conservation International (BCI) works hard to teach people that bats are shy and gentle.
4. The bats migrate from central Mexico each spring.
5. Bats use echoes to help find their way around in the dark.
6. Farmers like the bats because bats eat insects that hurt farmers' crops.

NOW I know why Austin's bats are so amazing!

Inferring

When we **infer** we use background knowledge with clues in the text to come up with our own ideas about what the author is trying to present.

To infer
- identify what you already know
- combine what you know with text clues to come up with your own ideas

Let's **Think** About **Reading!**

When I infer, I ask myself
- What do I already know?
- Which text clues are important?
- What is the author trying to present?

Inferring
The Unsinkable Wreck of the R.M.S. Titanic
by Robert D. Ballard and Rich Archbold

Facts and Details	My Inferences
The author's crew was the first in more than 70 years to "walk" on the Titanic's deck.	People must have been trying to reach the wreck for a long time!
There were not enough lifeboats for everyone on board the Titanic.	People must have thought the Titanic wouldn't sink. They were not prepared.
After the iceberg hit the Titanic, the captain "rushes from his cabin" to be told the news.	That must have been really scary and awful for him!
Few third-class passengers survived the sinking of the Titanic.	It seems like third-class passengers were considered less important than the wealthy passengers. That's sad.
The author says, "I found it hard to believe that only a thin film of sediment covered plates and bottles that had lain on the bottom for seventy-four years."	The author is amazed that so much of the Titanic is in good shape after all these years!

Something I learned from this selection ...
    People thought the Titanic in 1912
    was the most amazing ship ever.
    It was considered "unsinkable."

Monitor and Clarify

We **monitor comprehension** to check our understanding of what we've read. We **clarify** to find out why we haven't understood what we've read and to adjust comprehension.

To monitor and clarify
- use background knowledge
- try different strategies: ask questions, reread, or use text features and illustrations

Let's Think About Reading!

When I monitor and clarify, I ask myself
- Do I understand what I'm reading?
- What doesn't make sense?
- What strategies can I use?

Monitor and Clarify
Red Kayak
by Priscilla Cummings

When something doesn't make sense, I stop reading to clarify.

Notes on Red Kayak:

Confusing sentence: "I kept going, but toward the head of the creek, a marsh taken over by a patch of tall phragmites warned me of shallow water." Read sentence again.

What are phragmites?   Plants? Long grassy plants? Cattail things? Water plants?

(Looked up in dictionary--RIGHT! Phragmites are "common tall reeds.")

Confusing details about CPR after Brady rescues Ben. Help!—I don't know much about CPR. Read sentence more slowly. Got it!

Predict and Set Purpose

We **predict** to tell what might happen next in a story or article. The prediction is based on what has already happened. We **set a purpose** to guide our reading.

To predict and set a purpose
- preview the title, the author's name, and the illustrations or graphics
- identify why you're reading
- use what you already know to make predictions
- check and change your predictions based on new information

I predict the locations of the state capitals are based on their populations.

Let's Think About Reading!

When I predict and set a purpose, I ask myself
- What do I already know?
- What do I think will happen?
- What is my purpose for reading?

Predict and Set Purpose
Tripping Over the Lunch Lady
by Angela Johnson

My Purpose for Reading Is. . .
. . .to find out why this story is called Tripping Over the Lunch Lady.

My Predictions

1. I predict the story will be about a girl tripping in the cafeteria.
   right (wrong)   The story is about a girl wanting to square dance.

2. I predict Jinx is going to be a square dance star.
   right (wrong)   She sprains her ankle and can't dance.

3. Jinx says she will be the 5th grade school gym champion of the whole world, but I predict she won't be.
   (right) wrong   She is just exaggerating.

4. I predict something bad will happen to Jinx's best friend, Vic.
   (right) wrong   Vic's feet get twisted up in Jinx's feet, and Vic has to wear a cast.

5. I predict the kids in gym class will like square dancing after all.
   (right) wrong   They do!

Questioning

Questioning is asking good questions about important text information. Questioning takes place before, during, and after reading.

To question
- read with a question in mind
- stop, think, and record your questions as you read
- make notes when you find information
- check your understanding and ask questions to clarify

What does *arachnid* mean? Where do they fit in a food chain? Do tarantulas have to adapt to their environment to survive?

Let's Think About Reading!

When I question, I ask myself
- Have I asked a good question with a question word?
- What questions help me make sense of my reading?
- What does the author mean?

Questioning
Weslandia
by Paul Fleischman

As I read <u>Weslandia</u>, I wondered about the things that were happening and asked a lot of questions in my head.

Why does Wesley feel left out?
What kinds of plants does Wesley grow? How?
Where do the plants come from? Are they real?
How does Wesley learn to do all the things he does with the plants?
Why do Wesley's parents think Wesley seems happier at the end?

Then, I checked to see if I could answer my questions. There were a few I still couldn't answer:

<u>Where do the plants come from? Are they real?</u>
I am not sure where the plants come from, or if they're real. I think they are real, unless Wesley is pretending the whole thing.

<u>How does Wesley learn to do all things he does with the plants?</u>
I don't know, but it seems like Wesley is pretty smart, and maybe he studied plants. Maybe he looked up some things, like how to make clothes, in a book.

Story Structure

Story structure is the arrangement of a story from beginning to end. You can use this information to summarize the story.

To identify story structure
- note the conflict, or problem, at the beginning of a story
- track the rising action as conflict builds in the middle
- recognize the climax when the characters face the conflict
- identify how the conflict is resolved

Problem/Conflict

Rising Action

Resolution

Let's Think About Reading!

When I identify story structure, I ask myself
- What is the story's conflict or problem?
- How does the conflict build throughout the story?
- How is the conflict resolved in the end?
- How might this affect future events?

18

Story Structure
The Ch'i-lin Purse
by Linda Fang

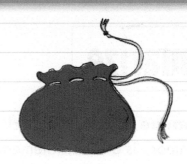

STORY STRUCTURE is the way a story is set up
from start to finish.

Conflict . . . the PROBLEM
Hsiang-ling is separated from her family by a terrible flood,
and goes from having a lot of money to having no money.

Rising Action . . . a SERIES OF EVENTS that leads to the climax
Hsiang-ling gets a job caring for a little boy. She discovers
the ch'i-lin purse she had given a poor bride years ago.

Climax . . . the TURNING POINT of the plot
Mrs. Lu, the boy's mother, figures out that
Hsiang-ling is the one who gave her the purse.

Resolution . . . when the problem is WORKED OUT
Mrs. Lu gives the purse back to Hsiang-ling and finds
Hsiang-ling's family. The families become close friends.

Summarize

We **summarize**, or retell, to check our understanding of what we've read. A summary is a brief statement—no more than a few sentences—and maintains a logical order.

To summarize fiction
- tell what happens in the story
- include the goals of the characters, how they try to reach them, and whether or not they succeed

To summarize nonfiction
- tell the main idea
- think about text structure and how the selection is organized

This blizzard is stalling rush hour traffic.

Let's Think About Reading!

When I summarize, I ask myself
- What is the story or selection about?
- In fiction, what are the characters' goals? Are they successful?
- In nonfiction, how is this information organized?

Summarize
The Fabulous Perpetual Motion Machine
by Don Abramson

I summarize what I read in my own words to make sure I understand. Here is my summary of The Fabulous Perpetual Motion Machine.

Lily and Carlos are twins who make something called a "perpetual motion machine" for a science project. They say the machine can run without power from anything else! Lily and Carlos' friends and family don't believe them at first, but then see the machine working.

Weird things start happening: people's watches stop running, the oven doesn't work, and lights flicker! In the end, the twins realize that the machine is stealing energy from everything else in their home!

Lily and Carlos turn off the machine and decide to invent something else for the science fair.

21

Text Structure

We use **text structure** to look for how the author has organized the text; for example, cause and effect, problem and solution, sequence, or compare and contrast. Analyze text structure before, during, and after reading to locate information.

To identify text structure

- before reading: preview titles, headings, and illustrations
- during reading: notice the organization
- after reading: recall the organization and summarize the text

First, teach your dog how to sit.

Then, teach him how to roll over.

Finally, teach him how to speak.

WOOF!

Let's **Think** About **Reading!**

When I identify text structure, I ask myself
- What clues do titles, headings, and illustrations provide?
- How is information organized?
- How does the organization help my understanding?

Text Structure
The Mystery of Saint Matthew Island
by Susan E. Quinlan

This article is about how all the reindeer died on Saint Matthew Island.
The author uses cause and effect to explain things. Examples:

Cause	Effect
Saint Matthew Island has no airport, and polar ice makes it hard to reach by boat.	It's hard to get to the island.
The reindeer have no natural enemies on the island.	The herd grows really fast.
Plants and other foods become hard to find.	Reindeers begin to lose weight and starve.
"In poor condition, and with little food to sustain them, disaster was inevitable."	"The harsh winter of 1963-64 spelled the end of the once healthy herd."

These causes and effects explain
why the reindeer disappeared.

23

Visualize

We **visualize** to form pictures in our minds as we read. This helps us monitor our comprehension.

To visualize

- combine what you already know with details from the text to make pictures in your mind
- use all of your senses to put yourself in the story or text

BLAZT OFF!

PLUMES OF ORANGE AND BLUE SMOKE FILL THE AIR. THE GROUND RUMBLES LIKE THUNDER. SUDDENLY, YOU'RE FLYING ABOVE THE GROUND AND INTO OUTER SPACE!

Let's Think About Reading!

When I visualize, I ask myself

- What do I already know?
- Which details create pictures in my mind?
- How can my senses put me in the story?

Visualize
At the Beach
by Lulu Delacre

When an author describes sights and smells in a story, I can form pictures in my mind. It's like I'm watching a movie! Sometimes I even draw the pictures on paper. These pictures help me understand what I'm reading.

What I "See" in My Mind

Fernando swimming
I see the bright hot sun and icy blue water. I see the other kids wading in the water too, and grown-ups tying hammocks to trees and cooking food on the beach. The beach in my mind looks a lot like the beach by my uncle's house!

Javi limping
I can see Javi limping after he steps on the sea urchin. Fernando is helping him walk back to the adults. Picturing Javi limping helps me understand how much his foot hurts, and why all the kids are worried about getting in trouble for going where they were not supposed to.

Luisa and Mari picking at their food
I can picture Luisa and Mari moving their food around on their plates but not eating anything because they feel guilty about lying to the grown-ups.

Envision It! | Visual Skills

Author's Purpose
Cause and Effect
Compare and Contrast
Draw Conclusions
Fact and Opinion
Generalize
Graphic Sources
Literary Elements
Main Idea and Details
Sequence
Author's Viewpoint and Bias
Classify and Categorize

Comprehension Skills

As you read,
- pay attention to the way the text is organized.
- think about the topic of the text.
- compare what you are reading with other things you have read.
- think like an author. What is the author's purpose for writing?

Comprehension skills are routines you use automatically in order to better understand what you read.

Ready to Try It? ▶

Author's Purpose

Entertain

Inform

Persuade

Express

An author writes for many purposes including to inform, entertain, persuade, or express. An author may have more than one purpose for writing.

How to Find Author's Purpose

The author's purpose is the main reason an author has for writing a selection. Is the author writing to persuade, to inform, to entertain, or to express ideas and feelings?

See It!

- Before you read, look at the photographs or illustrations. What do you see? How do the images make you feel? Why do you think the author chose those images?
- Are there a lot of subheads, text boxes, or other graphics in the selection? Is the text bright and colorful? What about the size and shape of the words? Does this give you an idea about the author's purpose?

Say It!

- Take turns reading aloud and listening to the first few paragraphs of a text with a partner. Discuss the kinds of words the author uses. Are the author's words persuasive, entertaining, informative, or expressive?
- Imagine how the author's voice might sound as you or your partner reads aloud. Would the author speak with a serious or lighthearted tone? Why do you think so?

Do It!

- Write the author's main ideas in your own words.
- Make a graphic organizer like the one below.

Ideas	Author's Purpose	Text
what they are how they are expressed	persuade inform entertain express	title and any heads facts and information fictional characters and plot pattern of ideas

- Pretend you are the author of the text, giving a "book talk" to the class. What would you say and why? Write and rehearse a short skit with a partner.

Skill

Strategy

Comprehension Skill

Author's Purpose

- The author's purpose is the main reason an author has for writing a selection.

- The author may wish to persuade, to entertain, to inform, or to express feelings or ideas.

- What the author says and the details he or she gives help you figure out the author's purpose.

- Use a graphic organizer like the one below to fill in the details the author provides that give clues to the purpose the author had for writing.

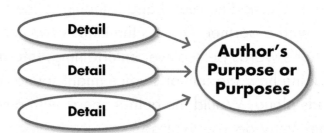

Comprehension Strategy

Monitor and Clarify

Good readers check, or monitor, their understanding as they read. As you read "The Trading Post," monitor your understanding by slowing down and reading a passage aloud.

The Trading Post

Imagine you are a Navajo living in the Southwest in the 1800s. Where would you go to catch up with friends *and* buy food and clothing? The mall? No! You would go to the trading post.

In those days, the Navajo would pack up their woven woolen blankets and rugs and jewelry, and travel several hours to the trading post. They would trade goods and talk with friends. Often these were the only times they saw neighbors.

Today these trading posts act mainly as banks and safes for the special needs of the Navajo. For example, where banks will not accept a sheep to secure a loan, a trading post will. The trading post understands that animals are a vital source of income for a Navajo family.

Other goods, such as ceremonial skins and baskets, are given to the trading post to store. These items are considered "live pawn" and are kept in the back of the store until the Navajo owner needs them. Tourists can't buy these items, but they can view them to learn about Navajo traditions. In this way, trading posts still act as the cultural hubs they were in the past.

Skill What do you think is the author's purpose? Is the author writing to entertain, express, or inform?

Strategy Pause here to monitor your comprehension. Reread the paragraph to clarify your understanding.

Skill Do you know more about trading posts now than you did before reading? Did the author achieve his or her purpose?

Your Turn!

Need a Review?
See *Envision It!* Skills and Strategies for additional help.

Ready to Try It?
Use what you've learned about author's purpose and monitoring and clarifying as you read other text.

Objectives

● Draw conclusions about texts and evaluate how well the author achieves his or her purpose.

Comprehension Skill

Author's Purpose

- The author's purpose is the reason or reasons an author has for writing. Most selections have one main purpose.

- An author may write to persuade you, to inform you, to entertain you, or to express ideas or feelings.

- Use a graphic organizer like the one below to decide on the author's purpose for writing "Before the Midnight Ride." Then think about how well the author achieved that purpose.

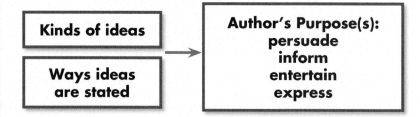

Comprehension Strategy

Background Knowledge

Active readers use what they already know to understand what they read. As you read, think about what you already know about people and events from your own life that are similar to those in the story. Making these types of connections will help you become a more active reader.

Before the Midnight Ride

Strategy Preview the title. What specific kind of knowledge would you need to understand what this selection will be about?

Paul Revere was born in December 1734 in Boston, Massachusetts. His childhood was much like that of other boys at the time.

When Paul was a teenager, he was paid to ring the bells at a church. At the same time, his father was teaching him to work with silver. Revere was a silversmith until he joined the army in 1756. After his army service, Revere married Sarah Orne and returned to his work.

In the 1760s and 1770s, trouble arose between the colonies and England. Revere joined a group called the Sons of Liberty. They believed the colonies should be free from England. In December 1773 he helped throw tea into Boston Harbor as a protest because the tea was taxed by England. This protest became known as the Boston Tea Party.

Skill What is the author's purpose for writing this selection?

After that, Revere became an express rider for the Massachusetts government. He rode a horse to bring news from Boston to the other colonies. He was at this job on that day in 1775, when his most famous ride took place.

Skill What does the author include in this selection that helped you determine the purpose for writing?

Your Turn!

 Need a Review?
See *Envision It!* Skills and Strategies for additional help.

 Ready to Try It?
Use what you've learned about author's purpose and background knowledge as you read other text.

Skill

Strategy

Comprehension Skill

Author's Purpose

- The author's purpose is the main reason an author writes. An author may write to persuade, to inform, to entertain, or to express ideas.

- You can use details from a text to determine an author's purpose.

- After reading a text, it is important to evaluate how well an author achieved his or her purpose.

- Use a graphic organizer like the one below to record the details about the author's purpose in "The United States in Space." Then, ask yourself if you think the author achieved his or her purpose.

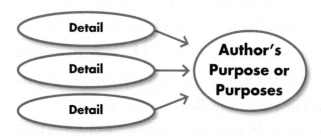

Comprehension Strategy

Monitor and Clarify

When you read nonfiction, you should always check your understanding of the text. One way to monitor understanding is to use your own knowledge about a topic. Another way is to make a list of important ideas in the text.

The United States
in Space

The space program in the United States, known to most people as NASA (the National Aeronautics and Space Administration), began in 1958. NASA was formed because the United States wanted to beat the Soviet Union in the "space race."

At first, the Soviet Union was ahead in the space race. The Soviets sent the first satellite into space in 1957. The United States did not send a satellite into space until 1958. The Soviet Union also sent the first person to orbit Earth in 1961. The United States did not send a person into orbit until 1962. That person was John Glenn. He orbited Earth three times.

Over time, the United States moved ahead in the space race. President John F. Kennedy gave NASA the goal of putting a person on the moon by the end of the 1960s. NASA was able to meet that goal. In 1969, Neil Armstrong was the first person to take a step on the moon. This feat helped the United States win the space race.

Skill After reading the first sentence, what do you think is the author's purpose for writing? What clue does the sentence provide?

Strategy How does using your own knowledge help you clarify this paragraph?

Skill What is the author's purpose in this text? Did the author achieve his or her purpose? Why or why not?

APOLLO 11

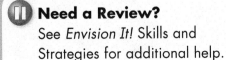

Your Turn!

❚❚ Need a Review?
See *Envision It!* Skills and Strategies for additional help.

▶ Ready to Try It?
Use what you've learned about author's purpose and monitoring and clarifying as you read other text.

Cause and Effect

An effect is something that happens. A cause is why that thing happens.

An effect sometimes has more than one cause. A cause sometimes has more than one effect.

READ THE LATEST... GRAVITY SUSPENDED

How to Identify Cause and Effect

A cause tells why something happened. An effect is what happened.

See It!

- Look for clue words in a text, such as *because, so, since,* and *for that reason.* They can tell about cause and effect.

- Make a picture in your mind as you read the following: *Nicole spilled a glass of water on the floor. Jeff walked into the room and slipped on the spill.* Identify the effect by asking, "What happened?" Identify the cause by asking, "Why did it happen?"

Say It!

- To understand cause and effect, ask yourself, "What happened?" and "Why did this happen?"

- Listen to a partner read sentences or paragraphs aloud. Listen for clue words, such as *because* or *so,* that tell about cause and effect.

Do It!

- Write an effect to this cause: *The temperature dropped to 40 degrees Fahrenheit when we were outside.*

- Make a graphic organizer such as the one below. (Remember that a cause can have more than one effect, and that an effect can have more than one cause. Add boxes to the graphic organizer if you need to.)

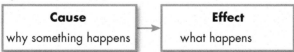

Cause	**Effect**
why something happens	what happens

- Write "what" and "why" questions about what you have read to a partner. Have your partner answer aloud or in writing.

Envision It! | Skill Strategy

Skill

Strategy

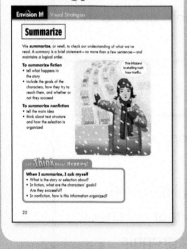

Comprehension Skill

🎯 Cause and Effect

● An effect is something that happens. A cause is the reason why something happens. A cause may have more than one effect, and an effect may have more than one cause.

● Clue words such as *because* and *since* can help you identify causes and effects. If there are no clue words, ask *Why did this happen? What happened as a result?*

● Analyze how causes and effects are organized to understand relationships.

● Use a graphic organizer like the one below to write three of the causes and effects from "The Real Thunder and Lightning."

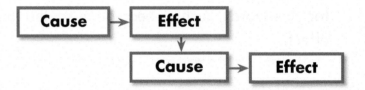

Comprehension Strategy

🎯 Summarize

Active readers summarize to check their understanding. As you read "The Real Thunder and Lightning," summarize the main ideas and leave out unimportant details so that you maintain the text's meaning.

The Real THUNDER and Lightning

Some tall tales and myths provide entertaining reasons for why things happen in nature. These stories are fun to read, but the real reasons can also be interesting.

The real cause of lightning is electrical charges. Inside a storm cloud, a strong positive electrical charge may form near the top, and a strong negative charge may form near the bottom. When these opposite charges flow toward each other, lightning flashes inside the cloud. When opposite charges flow from one cloud to another, lightning flashes between the clouds. When negative charges at the bottom of a cloud move down toward positive charges on Earth, lightning flashes from the cloud to the ground. Watch out!

Thunder happens only when there is lightning because lightning causes it. Thunder results from the rapid heating of the air along a lightning flash. The heated air expands. As a result, it creates a sound wave. Then the claps and rumbles of the thunder are heard.

Skill What clue word at the beginning of this paragraph lets you know that there is a cause-and-effect relationship here?

Skill What causes lightning that flashes from a cloud to the ground?

Strategy What ideas and details would you include in order to maintain meaning in a summary of this passage?

Your Turn!

Need a Review?
See *Envision It!* Skills and Strategies for additional help.

Ready to Try It?
Use what you've learned about cause and effect and summarizing as you read other text.

39

Objectives
● Analyze how the organization of a text affects the way ideas are related.

Envision It! | Skill Strategy

Skill

Envision It! Visual Skills

Cause and Effect

An effect is something that happens. A cause is why that thing happens.

An effect sometimes has more than one cause. A cause sometimes has more than one effect.

READ THE LATEST
GRAVITY
SUSPENDED

Strategy

Envision It! Visual Strategies

Text Structure

We use **text structure** to look for how the author has organized the text; for example, cause and effect, problem and solution, sequence, or compare and contrast. Analyze text structure before, during, and after reading to locate information.

To identify text structure
● before reading: preview titles, headings, and illustrations
● during reading: notice the organization
● after reading: recall the organization and summarize the text

First, teach your dog how to sit.

Then, teach him how to roll over.

Finally, teach him how to speak.

Let's **Think** about Reading!

When I identify text structure, I ask myself
● What does do titles, headings, and illustrations provide?
● How is information organized?
● How does the organization help my understanding?

22

READING STREET ONLINE
ENVISION IT! ANIMATIONS
www.ReadingStreet.com

Comprehension Skill

🎯 Cause and Effect

- An effect is something that happens. A cause is why it happens.

- Sometimes an author will use clue words such as *so* and *because* to show cause-and-effect relationships.

- The ideas in a text may be organized by causes and effects.

- Use a graphic organizer like the one below to show the causes of immigration. How do these causes help you understand the ideas presented in the text?

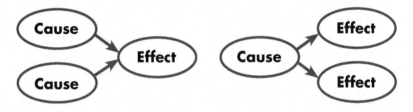

Comprehension Strategy

🎯 Text Structure

Text structure is the way a writer organizes a selection. A text may describe events in sequence, or in a cause-and-effect pattern. Active readers use text structure to help them understand what a selection is about. As you read, look for text structure.

COMING to the UNITED STATES

Imagine getting on a boat and leaving your homeland. You cross miles and miles of ocean to go live in a country you have never been to before. The people speak a different language, eat different foods, and wear different clothes.

If you did this, you would be an immigrant. Throughout U.S. history, many people have immigrated to this country. People continue to immigrate today. The largest number of immigrants arrived between 1880 and 1930. During this period, about twenty-seven million people came to the United States. Why?

Skill What clue word does the author use in this paragraph? Where do you think you will read about the causes?

In some cases, people came for freedom of religion. Some people came to escape wars or famine in their homelands. Other immigrants came to make money or pursue job opportunities. They left countries that had fewer jobs and fewer business opportunities than in the United States. These immigrants were willing to work hard to make better lives for themselves and their families.

Skill What are some of the many causes of immigration?

Strategy What kind of text structure does the author follow? Why do you think the author chose this structure?

Your Turn!

 Need a Review?
See *Envision It!* Skills and Strategies for additional help.

 Ready to Try It?
Use what you've learned about cause and effect and text structure as you read other text.

Objectives
● Summarize and paraphrase
information in a text. ● Analyze how
the organization of a text affects the
way ideas are related.

Skill

Strategy

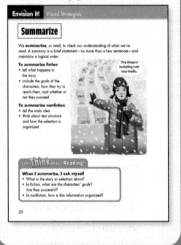

Comprehension Skill

Cause and Effect

- A cause (why something happens) may have several effects. An effect (what happens as a result of the cause) may have several causes.

- A text may be organized by cause-and-effect relationships among ideas.

- Sometimes clue words such as *since, as a result, caused, thus,* and *therefore* are used to show cause-and-effect relationships.

- Use a graphic organizer like the one below to help you record causes and effects. Then analyze how the cause-and-effect pattern in "Earth" influences the relationships among ideas in the text.

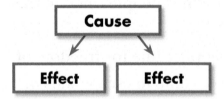

Comprehension Strategy

Summarize

Summarizing—telling what a story or article is about—helps you understand and remember what you read. It also helps you figure out main ideas and find important supporting details. As you summarize "Earth," it is important to maintain the meaning and logical order in the text.

EARTH

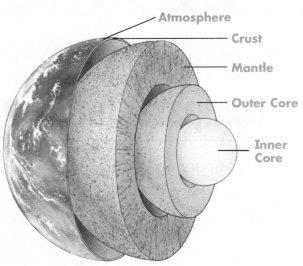

Atmosphere
Crust
Mantle
Outer Core
Inner Core

Until about sixty years ago, we didn't know much about the inside of the Earth. Then we invented drills called seismographs to measure movements below the surface. As scientists used these instruments to study what lies below ground, they learned more about what is inside the Earth.

Skill How does the cause-and-effect pattern in this paragraph show the relationship among ideas?

The Earth is made of three layers. The outer layer is the *crust,* the middle layer is the *mantle,* and the center layer is the *core.*

The crust is the thinnest layer. It is hard and can break. The crust is also the coolest layer.

The mantle is hotter and thicker than the crust. Even though the mantle does not get hot enough to melt, it does get hot enough for rocks to move. This movement causes volcanoes and earthquakes.

Skill What causes earthquakes and volcanoes? What clue word is used?

The core has two sections. The outer core is a liquid. The liquid spins as the Earth spins, causing the Earth's magnetic field. The inner core is hard rock. The core is the hottest layer of the Earth.

Strategy Summarize the text while maintaining its meaning and order.

Your Turn!

❚❚ Need a Review?
See the *Envision It!* Skills and Strategies for additional help.

▶ Ready to Try It?
Use what you've learned about cause and effect and summarizing as you read other text.

Compare and Contrast

To compare and contrast is to look for similarities and differences in things.

How to Compare and Contrast

When we compare things, we say what is similar about them. When we contrast things, we say what is different about them. During reading, we think about what is alike and what is different.

See It!

- Look at page 44. What does it tell you about comparing and contrasting?

- Look at the illustrations that go with a story you are reading. If the characters or various settings are pictured, compare and contrast them.

- Look for clues words such as *like, as,* and *same* that signal that two things are similar. Look for words such as *but, unlike,* and *different* to show differences.

Say It!

- Tell a partner how you are alike and different from a family member. For example: *My brother is loud and talkative, but I am shy and quiet. However, we both like to play baseball.*

- Name an item in the classroom. Have a partner tell you one thing in the classroom that is similar to that object, and one thing that is different. Take turns naming things.

Do It!

- A Venn diagram is helpful when you want to tell how things are alike or different. However, it's not the only graphic organizer you can use to make comparisons. Try this one, below:

- With your teacher, gather small items around the classroom that you can compare and contrast. How are the things you've chosen alike? How are they different?

Objectives
● Evaluate the effects of sensory details, imagery, and figurative language in literary text.

Skill

Strategy

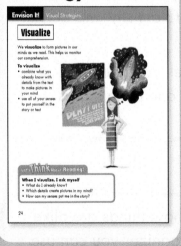

Comprehension Skill

Compare and Contrast

- When writers compare and contrast, they tell how things are alike or different.

- Words such as *same, unlike, but,* and *although* are clues that sometimes show comparisons and contrasts.

- Sometimes writers do not use clue words when they compare and contrast things.

- Use a graphic organizer like the one below to compare and contrast Ryan's actions.

Responsible	Not Responsible

Comprehension Strategy

Visualize

Active readers look for sensory details to create pictures in their minds as they read. The sights and smells described by the author help you visualize the story. As you read, think about the impact sensory details and imagery have on the story.

Ryan & Jonah

Ryan was babysitting his brother, Jonah. He started a movie, set Jonah down, and told him to stay put. Then he began sorting his baseball cards. After a while, he looked up. Where was Jonah? Ryan dashed around the living room and then through the whole house. Usually Jonah liked to sit and watch a whole movie, but now he wasn't there.

Skill What contrast is signaled by the word *but*?

Then he noticed the open back door and ran outside. Just then, Jonah fell in the swimming pool. Ryan ran over and pulled him out. As the boys hurried into the house, Ryan said, "Don't tell Mom what happened. Let's get you some dry clothes."

Just then, the boys' mom walked in and asked why Jonah was soaked. "He got his clothes dirty, and I tried to clean them," said Ryan. Mom took off Jonah's wet clothes and shoes. She wrapped a towel around the shaking little boy. Ryan looked at Jonah's wet shoes and said, "I wasn't watching, and Jonah fell into the pool. I pulled him out, but we were scared to tell you."

Skill Ryan gives his mother two explanations. In what ways are the explanations alike? In what ways are they different?

Strategy How do the imagery and sensory details in this story affect your understanding of the story?

Mom hugged each of the boys. "Jonah could have drowned! Thank goodness you found him in time, and everyone is OK."

Your Turn!

 Need a Review?
See *Envision It!* Skills and Strategies for additional help.

Ready to Try It?
Use what you've learned about comparing and contrasting and visualizing as you read other text.

Objectives

• Describe specific events in the story or novel that result in or hint at future events.

Skill

Strategy

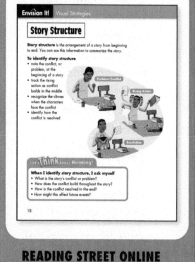

Comprehension Skill

Compare and Contrast

- When you compare and contrast things, you tell how they are alike or different.

- Sometimes clue words point out comparisons and contrasts, but not always.

- You can compare and contrast things within a story, or one story with another.

- Use a graphic organizer like the one below to help you write a folk tale. Include ideas that are similar to and different from "Ah Tcha's Leaves."

Similarities in Text	Differences in Text	Compare with What I Know

Comprehension Strategy

Story Structure

Active readers pay attention to story structure. Generally, authors identify the problem of the main character at the start. They work through the problem as the action rises in the middle, and then solve it with the climax and outcome. Authors also use story incidents to foreshadow or give rise to future events.

Ah Tcha's Leaves

Ah Tcha was a wealthy man. He owned seven farms and seven rice mills in China. He paid his workers in gold, but some grumbled about the hard work. An old woman, Nu Wu, complained the most.

One night, Ah Tcha found mice eating his rice. A cat slept nearby. Ah Tcha threw a giant sack at the cat to wake her. Poof! The cat changed into Nu Wu. She was angry with Ah Tcha. She cried, "You will sleep eleven hours out of every twelve!"

Ah Tcha slept nearly every day and night. He lost everything and became poor. One night, Nu Wu pounded on Ah Tcha's door, waking him. She wanted food. Ah Tcha had only leaves from a bush by his house, so he tossed them into hot water. Nu Wu grumbled, but drank her cup and left.

Ah Tcha drank a cup. He did not fall asleep! He smiled. "Nu Wu thanked me by charming the leaves to banish my sleepiness."

Ah Tcha sold the leaves. He planted extra bushes and became rich. Throughout China, people asked for the "drink of Ah Tcha" or "Tcha." In time, *Tcha* became *Tay*, and finally *tea*.

Skill How is Ah Tcha's current situation different from his situation at the beginning of the story?

Skill Find two times Nu Wu changed Ah Tcha's life. How were those times alike? How were they different?

Strategy How do the events in the story give rise to the ending?

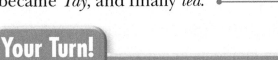

Your Turn!

⏸ Need a Review?
See *Envision It!* Skills and Strategies for additional help.

▶ Ready to Try It?
Use what you've learned about comparing and contrasting and story structure as you read other text.

49

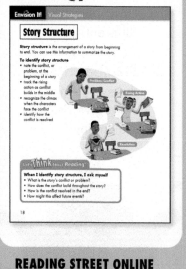
Comprehension Skill

Compare and Contrast

• When writers compare and contrast things, they tell how those things are alike or different. Words such as *same*, *also*, *before*, *although*, and *however* are clues that things are being compared and contrasted.

• You can compare and contrast different things you read about with one another.

• Use a graphic organizer like the one below to record comparisons and contrasts that you find in "Andrew's Wish."

Beginning	End

Comprehension Strategy

Story Structure

Active readers notice story structure, including the problems characters face and the rising action, climax, and outcome. Authors use story incidents to advance plots and give rise to future events. After reading "Andrew's Wish," describe the incidents that advanced the story or foreshadowed the events at the end.

Andrew's Wish

Andrew had always dreamed of his very own mountain bike. Like his friends, Andrew loved riding on the trails. However, sometimes he chose not to ride because he hated having to borrow one of his friends' bikes.

As Andrew walked home from school one day, he noticed a frog following him. When he asked what the frog wanted, the frog said, "I want to grant you a wish because you did not step on me." Andrew immediately asked for a bike. The frog said he could give Andrew a magic bicycle that only Andrew could see. Whenever someone else got close, the bike would disappear. Andrew agreed to this because he wanted a bike so much.

Later, Andrew rode his bike alone. He had a lot of fun, but he missed his friends. The next day, Andrew rode his magic bike to meet his friends. When he met them, the bike disappeared. Andrew realized that having a bike was not as important as having friends, so he returned the magic bike to the frog. The next day, Andrew happily borrowed a bike and went riding with his friends.

Skill What comparisons and contrasts can you find in this paragraph?

Skill Compare Andrew's feelings about borrowing a bike at the beginning of the story to those he had at the end of the story.

Strategy Identify and explain the events in the story that gave rise to the story's ending.

Your Turn!

⏸ Need a Review?
See *Envision It!* Skills and Strategies for additional help.

▷ Ready to Try It?
Use what you've learned about comparing and contrasting and story structure as you read other text.

Draw Conclusions

When we draw conclusions, we make decisions
or form an opinion about what we read.

How to Draw Conclusions

When we draw conclusions, we form an opinion by combining our own background knowledge with the facts and details stated in a text.

See It!

- Look at page 52. What details do you notice? What conclusions can you make about what is happening?

- Picture in your mind someone who is mad, happy, sad, or excited. What kinds of clues do they give you about their mood?

Say It!

- Talk about conclusions you make with a partner. Ask "Why is this happening?" while examining details from the story and from what you know from your own life. Ask "Is this the only logical conclusion?"

- Share with a small group what you already know about the subject you're reading about. Each group member should share their knowledge.

Do It!

- Make a graphic organizer like the one below to help you draw conclusions.

- Write a brief mystery story where the main character has to draw a conclusion based on clues. Add facts and details that help the character solve the mystery.

- Practice drawing conclusions by writing "Who or What Am I?" questions for a partner.

Objectives

● Ask different types of questions about a text. ● Monitor and adjust comprehension using a variety of strategies.

Skill

Strategy

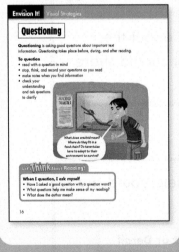

Comprehension Skill

Draw Conclusions

• A conclusion is a decision you make after thinking about the details of what you read.

• Your own prior knowledge can help you draw conclusions. When you draw a conclusion, be sure it makes sense and is supported by what you have read.

• Use the text and a graphic organizer like the one below to help you draw a conclusion about Jeff.

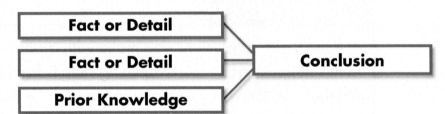

Comprehension Strategy

Questioning

As you read, it is important to ask questions. Begin reading with a question in mind and make notes when you find information that answers your question. You can ask an interpretive question, which will help you explain something in a story or text. Your answers can help you monitor and clarify your comprehension of a story.

54

THE GO-CART

The summer had been downright boring. Nothing extraordinary had occurred. Then Jeff read an ad in the local newspaper: "Go-Cart Race Next Month! Win $1,000!" He decided that he *had* to enter the race.

"But Jeff, you don't own a go-cart," his father said.

The newspaper noted that the go-cart had to be homemade. Jeff had been saving his allowance, and he had enough money for the plans and parts for the go-cart.

"But Jeff, you've never built anything," his mother said.

Jeff set about his building task. He read the instructions that came with the go-cart kit carefully. If something was confusing or hard to understand, he called the hardware store and asked for a clerk to explain. Every day he toiled on his go-cart, and every night it was that much closer to being finished.

Finally, the day of the race arrived. Jeff put on his helmet and revved his engine. The announcer roared, "On your mark! Get set! Go!" And Jeff, who had never raced a go-cart before, was off!

> **Skill** Draw a conclusion about why you think Jeff *had* to enter the race.

> **Strategy** What kind of person do you think Jeff is?

> **Skill** Draw a conclusion about how you think Jeff felt as he revved his engine.

Your Turn!

❚❚ Need a Review?
See *Envision It!* Skills and Strategies for additional help.

▷ Ready to Try It?
Use what you've learned about drawing conclusions and questioning as you read other text.

55

Envision It! | Skill Strategy

Skill

Strategy

Comprehension Skill

Draw Conclusions

- A conclusion is a reasonable decision you make after you think about the facts or details you read.

- Drawing conclusions may also be called making inferences.

- You can also use your prior knowledge to help you draw conclusions.

- Use a graphic organizer like the one below to help you draw conclusions about the information the author presents in "The History of Gymnastics."

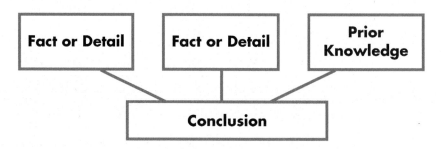

Comprehension Strategy

Visualize

Active readers visualize, or make pictures in their mind. Visualizing can help you understand a text. Look for details that will help you visualize what is happening.

The History of Gymnastics

Early Greek teachers were the first to teach gymnastics both for athletes and for everyone else. More than three thousand years ago, every Greek student would train in gymnastics. People thought that exercise taught the body and mind to work together.

Skill What conclusion can you draw about how Greeks thought about themselves and their bodies?

The Greeks taught three different kinds of gymnastics. One kind helped people stay strong and in good shape. Another helped people become strong and fit for sports. A third was used to train men for military service. Roman soldiers would also train in gymnastics.

Strategy How do the details in this paragraph help you visualize the information being presented?

Over time, people in Europe began to learn and enjoy gymnastics. During the 1970s, people all over the world watched the gymnasts at the Olympics.

At first, Americans did not enjoy gymnastics as much as the Europeans. They liked watching games instead, such as basketball or baseball. However, beginning in the 1970s, gymnastics became popular in the United States as well.

Skill Why do you think gymnastics started to become popular during the 1970s? Explain your conclusion.

Your Turn!

 Need a Review?
See *Envision It!* Skills and Strategies for additional help.

 Ready to Try It?
Use what you've learned about drawing conclusions and visualizing as you read other text.

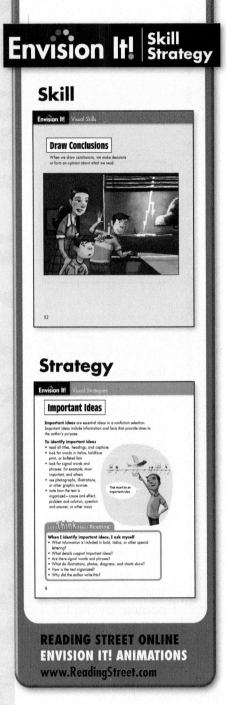

Envision It! | Skill Strategy

Skill

Envision It! Visual Skills

Draw Conclusions

When we draw conclusions, we make decisions or form an opinion about what we read.

52

Strategy

Envision It! Visual Strategies

Important Ideas

Important ideas are essential ideas in a nonfiction selection. Important ideas include information and facts that provide clues to the author's purpose.

To identify important ideas
• read all titles, headings, and captions
• look for words in italics, boldface print, or bulleted lists
• look for signal words and phrases: for example, most important, and others
• use photographs, illustrations, or other graphic sources
• note how the text is organized—cause and effect, problem and solution, question and answer, or other ways

This must be an important idea.

Let's Think about Reading!

When I identify important ideas, I ask myself
• What information is included in bold, italics, or other special lettering?
• What details support important ideas?
• Are there signal words and phrases?
• What do illustrations, photos, diagrams, and charts show?
• How is the text organized?
• Why did the author write this?

8

**READING STREET ONLINE
ENVISION IT! ANIMATIONS**
www.ReadingStreet.com

Comprehension Skill

Draw Conclusions

- Active readers make decisions based on evidence in the text or on their own background knowledge.

- When you form an idea or opinion about a text, you are drawing a conclusion.

- Examine your own conclusions as you read. Ask yourself if you can support them with facts from the text or facts you already know.

- Use a graphic organizer like the one below to draw conclusions about "The Mystery of the Monarchs."

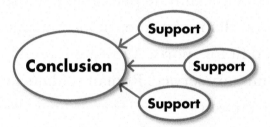

Comprehension Strategy

Important Ideas

Good readers pay close attention to the important ideas in a piece of writing. Important ideas are the details and essential information that help you understand what an author is writing about.

The Mystery of the Monarchs

Have you ever seen the orange-and-black butterflies known as monarchs? If you have, it was probably autumn. The butterflies were migrating through your area on their way to Mexico.

Skill Draw a conclusion about why butterflies migrate to Mexico.

All monarch butterflies spend the winter months in forests in Mexico, where it is warm. They fly there in large groups. In the spring these monarchs repeat the same flight in the other direction. They fly back to the North as far as Canada and lay eggs along the way. Then they die.

But when those eggs hatch, a new generation of butterflies is born. When another autumn comes, they take off for Mexico. They repeat the flight path of the original butterflies, and, amazingly, they fly to the same forests and sometimes the exact same trees where their parents came from previously. Think about it: they fly to the same forests and trees and they've never been there before!

Strategy What information does this paragraph tell you? Is it important to understand these ideas to know what the author is writing about?

Scientists think the butterflies begin their journey because of the position of the sun in the sky as the seasons change. But for now, though, no one can explain how the butterflies know where to go. That remains the "mystery of the monarchs."

Skill What conclusion can you draw about ongoing study of the monarch butterflies?

Your Turn!

Need a Review?
See *Envision It!* Skills and Strategies for additional help.

Ready to Try It?
Use what you've learned about drawing conclusions and important ideas as you read other text.

Fact and Opinion

A fact is something that can be proved true or false.
An opinion can't be proved.

How to Identify Fact and Opinion

You can check facts by using prior knowledge, asking an expert, or checking a reference. A statement of opinion tells someone's ideas or feelings and should be supported by good logic.

See It!

- Look at page 60. What fact is being stated? How do you know that this is a fact? What opinion is being expressed? How do you know?

- Look at reference books such as encyclopedias, textbooks, or official Web sites to tell if something is true or false. Some sentences contain both facts and opinions.

Say It!

- Tell a partner one fact and one opinion about something. Your partner should be able to identify what is fact and what is opinion.

- Tell a partner a statement of opinion, such as *Basketball is the best sport to play.* Have your partner change your statement to one that either states a fact, or adds facts and logic to support the opinion.

Do It!

- Use a graphic organizer such as the one below to help you organize valid and faulty opinions in a text. (Note: *faulty* means "weak" or "illogical.")

Statement of Opinion	Support	Valid or Faulty?

- Write a paragraph that tells about what you did in the morning before school. Be sure to include facts and opinions.

Comprehension Skill

Fact and Opinion

- You can prove a statement of fact true or false. You can do this by using your own knowledge, asking an expert, or checking a reference source.

- A statement of opinion gives ideas or feelings, not facts. It cannot be proved true or false.

- A sentence may contain both a statement of fact and a statement of opinion.

- Use a graphic organizer like the one below to help you determine and verify facts in "A Special League."

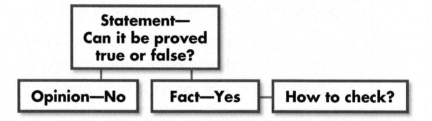

Comprehension Strategy

Questioning

As you read, ask yourself questions. You can ask a literal question, which can be answered by looking at or recalling information directly in the text. The answers to your questions can help you recall and understand what you read.

A Special League

African Americans have played baseball since the sport began. For many years, however, they were not allowed to play on the same team as white players.

In 1882, the first African American teams were formed. Unlike earlier players, these players were paid to play, because they were more fun to watch.

Skill Does this sentence contain a fact and an opinion?

The National Negro League (NNL) was founded in 1920. Another league, the Eastern Colored League, was founded in 1923. These leagues gave talented athletes the chance to play and gave fans the chance to see the best baseball players of all time.

Strategy Do you have any literal questions to ask here? If so, write them down.

The NNL became very popular in the 1930s. From then until 1950, teams played in the East–West All-Star Game, attended by up to forty thousand fans! Yet things were not so easy for African American players. They had to travel more often and play more games than white players. They made less money. In some places they were refused hotel rooms.

In 1947, professional baseball became integrated. That year, African Americans were allowed to play with whites in the major leagues. Meanwhile, television was starting to show baseball games. These events eventually led to the end of the NNL.

Skill What could you use to verify this article's facts?

Your Turn!

Need a Review?
See *Envision It!* Skills and Strategies for additional help.

Ready to Try It?
Use what you've learned about fact and opinion and questioning as you read other text.

Envision It! | Skill Strategy

Skill

Strategy

Comprehension Skill

🎯 Fact and Opinion

- You can prove statements of fact true or false by verifying them with your own knowledge, asking an expert, or checking a reference source.

- An opinion gives ideas or feelings, not facts, and cannot be proved true or false.

- A sentence may contain both a statement of fact and a statement of opinion.

- Use a graphic organizer like the one below to help you determine and verify facts in "Dinosaurs."

Statement— Can it be proved true or false?		
Opinion—No	Fact—Yes	How to check?

Comprehension Strategy

🎯 Predict and Set Purpose

Active readers try to predict what they will learn when they read a nonfiction article. This helps them establish a purpose for why they are reading the article. Previewing an article is a good way to predict what you will be reading and to establish your purpose for reading. Establishing a purpose for reading can help you understand a text.

DINOSAURS

By far the most fascinating creatures ever to walk the Earth were the dinosaurs. Their name comes from two Greek words that mean "terrible lizard." When you see drawings or models of certain dinosaurs, it is very easy to understand how they got their name.

Skill There are two statements of opinion in this paragraph. Identify one of them.

Types of dinosaurs Some dinosaurs were herbivores, meaning that they ate only plants. Apatosaurus and Iguanodon were herbivores. Other dinosaurs were carnivores, or meat eaters. The most feared dinosaur of all, Tyrannosaurus, was a carnivore.

Strategy Preview the title and the headings. What will this article be about? What is your purpose for reading it?

Dinosaur characteristics Dinosaurs were marked by special body features. Stegosaurus had armor it used for protection. Pterosaur had wings like a bat's. Tyrannosaurus had strong back legs but short, weak front ones.

Skill Which statements are facts in this paragraph? What could you use to check whether they are true or false?

What happened to the dinosaurs? No one knows for sure, though there are several ideas about why they disappeared. Some of these ideas are as interesting as the dinosaurs themselves.

Your Turn!

 Need a Review?
See *Envision It!* Skills and Strategies for additional help.

 Ready to Try It?
Use what you've learned about fact and opinion and predicting and setting a purpose as you read other text.

Objectives

● Identify the facts in a text and prove that they are facts.

Skill

Strategy

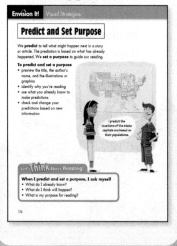

Comprehension Skill

Fact and Opinion

● Statements of fact can be proved true or false. You can verify facts through established methods, such as using prior knowledge, asking an expert, or checking a reference.

● Statements of opinion are personal judgments that cannot be proved true or false. Determine if opinions are either valid or faulty by using your prior knowledge.

● Use a graphic organizer like the one below to help you record opinions and determine and verify facts in "How Blimps Are Used."

Statement of Opinion	Support	Valid or Faulty?

Comprehension Strategy

Predict and Set Purpose

Active readers try to predict what they will learn when they read nonfiction. Predicting as you preview the article can also help you set a purpose for what you are reading. After you read, see whether your prediction was correct.

How Blimps Are Used

There is no better outdoor advertisement than the blimp. These flying billboards carry advertising messages hundreds and thousands of feet in the air, where they can be viewed by hundreds and thousands of people at once. These flying machines have appeared in the skies for more than eighty years.

In 1925, the American tire company Goodyear built its first blimp. It was a huge success. Goodyear built almost three hundred blimps, all promoting their products. They are often seen on TV sports programs. Cameras on board give viewers aerial shots of the action.

These blimps are faster than most ocean ships. In fact, the U.S. Navy used them during the Second World War. Large enough to carry equipment and stay in the air for days at a time, they are also used by law enforcement officers.

Because blimps have the best safety record of any flying vehicle today, they are used to cover many special events. Today, tourists also use them. There is no better way to see the African plains than by floating above them. A ride in a blimp is truly a unique adventure.

Strategy Preview the title. What do you think this article will be about? What purpose for reading will you be setting?

Skill Which statements in this paragraph are facts? How would you go about verifying them?

Skill Based on your own knowledge, is this statement of opinion valid or faulty? Why?

Your Turn!

Need a Review?
See *Envision It!* Skills and Strategies for additional help.

Ready to Try It?
Use what you've learned about facts and opinions and predicting and setting purpose as you read other text.

Generalize

To generalize is to make a broad statement or rule that applies to many examples.

How to Generalize

To make a generalization, look at a number of different examples of something and use your prior knowledge to decide what all of the examples have in common.

See It!

- As you read, look for clue words that might signal a generalization, such as *many*, *most*, *usually*, *never*, *all*, or *few*.

- Look around the classroom for objects you can make a generalization about. When you have chosen an object, examine it and make a generalization about it. Remember to ask yourself if your generalization can be supported by facts.

Say It!

- When you find a statement in your reading that makes a generalization, read it aloud. With a partner, talk about why this is a generalization.

- Ask a partner if he or she can make a generalization about something in your reading, using key words such as *all, most, many,* or *none*.

- What kinds of generalizations have you heard? Discuss with a partner or small group.

Do It!

- Use a graphic organizer such as the one below to help you make generalizations as you read. When making a generalization, ask yourself if it is supported by facts.

Support from Article	→	Generalization	←	Support from Article

- Bring a notebook to lunch or to the playground, and look for generalizations you can make about certain foods, games, plants, and so on.

Skill

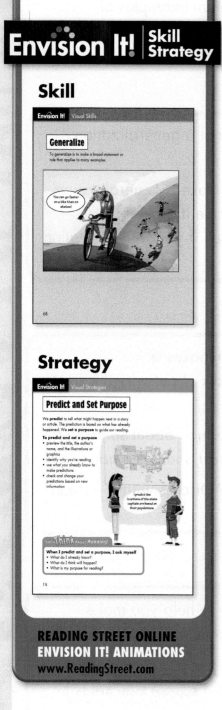

Strategy

Comprehension Skill

Generalize

- To generalize is to make a broad statement or inference that applies to several examples.

- Active readers make generalizations about story characters as they read. They support their generalizations using evidence from the text as well as their own background knowledge.

- Use a graphic organizer like the one below to help you make a generalization about Victor's character and to use textual evidence to support your understanding about Victor.

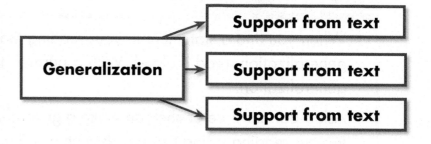

Comprehension Strategy

Predict and Set Purpose

As you read, it is important to make predictions. You can check your predictions during and after reading. Your predictions will help you set your purpose for reading as you read to see if you were right. This will help you recall and understand what you read.

The School Dance

Victor looked at himself in the mirror. He was wearing a sport coat and a new pair of shoes. "I think I look okay," he thought, "but what if the other kids don't think so?"

Victor was going to the Autumn Dance at school. He was looking forward to seeing his friends, but he was a little nervous about dancing. "What if I look goofy?" Victor worried.

Victor had asked his mother those questions. "You'll be fine," his mother said. "Just go and have fun."

At the gym, Victor saw that all the students were standing against the walls of the large room. Music was playing but no one was dancing. In fact, most kids were looking at their shoes. Then Victor spotted Nadia, his neighbor. He'd known Nadia since they were in second grade! At the same time, Nadia rushed up to Victor and said, "Let's dance! Someone's got to get things started."

Victor felt weird, but he and Nadia started dancing in the middle of the room anyway. Slowly, other kids came out to dance too. Soon everyone was laughing and having fun.

Skill What generalizations can you infer about Victor from what he says in the text?

Strategy What do you predict will happen to Victor at the dance?

Skill What generalization can you make about the other kids from the way they are acting?

Your Turn!

❚❚ Need a Review?
See *Envision It!* Skills and Strategies for additional help.

▶ Ready to Try It?
Use what you've learned about generalizations and predicting and setting a purpose as you read other text.

71

Envision It! | Skill Strategy

Skill

Strategy

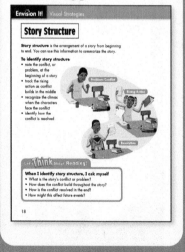

Comprehension Skill

Generalize

• To generalize is to make a broad statement or rule that applies to several examples.

• Active readers pay close attention to what authors tell them about story characters and make generalizations about those characters as they read.

• A generalization should be supported with evidence from the text.

• Use a graphic organizer like the one below to make a generalization about April. Use the story to back up your generalization.

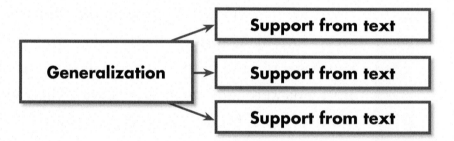

Comprehension Strategy

Story Structure

Active readers notice story structure. They note the problem characters face and the rising action, climax, and outcome. Generally, authors show the problem, or conflict, at the start. The characters work through the conflict as the action rises, and then solve it in the outcome.

First Day
Without Joy

The sunny morning seemed gloomy to April. Yesterday, Joy had moved from the house next door. April was miserable as she imagined her first day of school without Joy.

Skill Make a generalization about April's character. What supports your generalization?

Joy and April had been inseparable. They had studied together, walked to school together, and eaten lunch together. Today, April walked to school alone. Would she eat lunch alone?

Strategy What is the character's conflict? How do you think the character will resolve the problem?

At school, the teacher introduced a new girl named Blanca. When the lunch bell rang, students rushed out the door. April was the last to leave. Her feet felt weighted as she moved toward the cafeteria.

In the cafeteria, everyone was eating with a friend. Where would April eat? She spotted Blanca alone near the door. *She must feel alone* thought April.

Skill Make a generalization about the students at April's school. What supports your generalization?

"Will you eat with me, Blanca?" April asked. Blanca's face lit up, and they sat down.

"Where do you live?" asked April.

"My address is 128 Oak Street."

"That's down the street from me!"

The girls walked home together. "What a gorgeous, sunny day!" April said.

Your Turn!

Need a Review?
See *Envision It!* Skills and Strategies for additional help.

Ready to Try It?
Use what you've learned about generalizations and story structure as you read other text.

Skill

Strategy

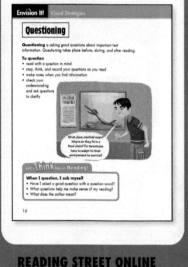

Comprehension Skill

Generalize

- To generalize means to make an inference that applies to several examples.

- Sometimes authors make generalizations in their writing. Clue words such as *all, many,* and *most* can signal generalizations.

- *Valid generalizations* are supported by the text or logic. *Faulty generalizations* are not supported by the text or logic.

- Use a graphic organizer like the one below to determine if the generalization in the final paragraph in "The Gold Rush" is *valid* or *faulty.*

Generalization	**Support from Article**
	Support from Article
	Support from Article

Comprehension Strategy

Questioning

As you read, it is important to ask different types of questions. When you ask an evaluative question, you make a judgment about what you read. Begin reading by asking a question about the author's purpose. Ask yourself why an author chose to write something.

THE GOLD RUSH

Abraham Lincoln described the western United States in the mid-1800s as the "treasure house of the nation." Why? People had found large, abundant amounts of gold, silver, and other precious metals there.

The first large amount, or lode, of gold was found near the Sacramento River in California in 1848 by John Sutter and James Marshall. They tried to hide their discovery, but soon people found out. By 1849, about eighty thousand people were in the area searching for gold. Many Americans had caught gold fever!

A lode of silver was found in 1859 in Nevada. Discovered on a property owned by Henry Comstock, it became known as the Comstock Lode. Many people got rich from the Comstock Lode. Grubby miners turned into instant millionaires. George Hearst and a group of friends made ninety thousand dollars in two months. One deposit, known as The Big Bonanza, produced more than one million dollars worth of gold and silver.

Many towns were built and destroyed by the Gold Rush. Towns such as Virginia City, Nevada, and Cripple Creek, Colorado, sprang up almost overnight. While the gold or silver lasted, the towns were successful. When the gold or silver was used up, however, many towns became deserted.

Skill Notice the three examples in the last sentence. From them, what generalization did Abraham Lincoln make about the West in the mid-1800s?

Strategy Evaluate what you have learned about the Gold Rush. Do you have any other questions? Will your questions help you recall what you've read?

Skill What generalization is made in this paragraph? Is this generalization valid or faulty? How can you tell?

AN ACCOUNT OF
CALIFORNIA,
AND THE
WONDERFUL GOLD REGIONS.

A New Arrival at the Gold Diggings.

WITH A DESCRIPTION OF
The Different Routes to California;
Information about the Country, and the Ancient and Modern Discoveries of Gold;
How to Test Precious Metals; Accounts of Gold Hunters;
TOGETHER WITH MUCH OTHER
Useful Reading for those going to California, or having Friends there.
ILLUSTRATED WITH MAPS AND ENGRAVINGS.

BOSTON:
PUBLISHED BY J. B. HALL, 60 CORNHILL.
For Sale at Holmes's Publication Rooms, 651 Cornhill.

Price, 12½ cents.

Your Turn!

❚❚ Need a Review?
See *Envision It!* Skills and Strategies for additional help.

▶ Ready to Try It?
Use what you've learned about generalizations and questioning as you read other text.

Graphic Sources

A graphic source shows information in a way that the reader can see.

Table

A table is a box, square, or rectangle that contains information in rows and columns.

Bar Graph

A bar graph uses horizontal and vertical lines to compare information.

Map

A map is a drawing of a place and shows where something is or where something happened.

Diagram

A diagram is a drawing, usually with parts that are labeled.

How to Use Graphic Sources

Graphic sources include charts, tables, graphs, maps, illustrations, and photographs. These features can help you understand information or predict what your reading will be about.

See It!

- Look at pages 76–77. What do you notice? What do the images and text tell you about how graphic sources make information easier to understand?

- During reading, scan the text for graphic sources that help you understand the topic. Look for captions underneath photographs, as well as charts, illustrations, or underlined or boldface words.

- Pick a graphic source in your reading, such as a map or diagram, to examine in depth. What kind of information does it show?

Say It!

- Take a few minutes to review a graphic source you come across while reading, and then explain the information to a partner. Does it make sense? If you or your partner become confused, look back over it together.

- Skim graphic sources before reading. Then tell a partner what you notice. This can help prepare you for reading the main text.

- While examining graphic sources, ask yourself or a partner, "What is the purpose of this graphic? Why would the author choose to include it?"

Do It!

- Create your own graphic source to go with something you've written or read. You might choose to create a map, bar graph, text box, or illustration with a caption. Be sure your graphic sources are properly labeled and relate to, or tell more about, your topic.

- Write a brief paragraph that tells about a favorite place. Include a graphic source with your paragraph, such as a labeled illustration of the place or a map of how to get there.

Skill

Strategy

READING STREET ONLINE
ENVISION IT! ANIMATIONS
www.ReadingStreet.com

Comprehension Skill

Graphic Sources

- A graphic source, such as a picture, diagram, or chart, organizes information and helps you understand what you read.

- Before reading, preview the graphic sources in a selection to help you gain an overview of the text's contents.

- As you read, compare the information in the text with the graphic source.

- Use a graphic organizer like the one below as you read "Computer Art and What It Takes." As you read, use the graphics to locate and interpret information.

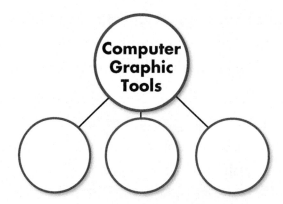

Comprehension Strategy

Important Ideas

When you read, try to identify the important ideas of a selection. The important ideas are the essential information, facts, and details that help you understand what an author is writing about.

80

Computer Art
AND WHAT IT TAKES

These days, computers can create art that you find in video games or on TV. This type of art is called computer graphics.

It does not take much to create a computer graphics system. Graphics software allows you to create the pictures. A computer hard drive stores the graphics, or pictures, and lets you work with them. A monitor shows you the pictures.

You also need a mouse and a keyboard to input commands. Equipment, such as a digital pad, a camera, a scanner, or a light pen, may be needed to input pictures. If you want to make a copy of the pictures on paper, you will need a printer too.

Skill Preview the picture below. What does it tell you about the article's contents?

Skill Which items mentioned in the text are shown in the picture below?

Strategy What is the most important idea of this paragraph?

Your Turn!

Need a Review?
See *Envision It!* Skills and Strategies for additional help.

Ready to Try It?
Use what you've learned about graphic sources and important ideas as you read other text.

Skill

Strategy

Comprehension Skill

🎯 Graphic Sources

- A graphic source, such as a picture, diagram, or chart, organizes information and makes it easy to see. Graphic sources help you understand what you read.

- Before reading, preview the graphic sources in a selection to help you gain an idea of the article's contents.

- As you read, compare the information in the text with the graphic source.

- Use a graphic organizer like the one below to help you use the graphics from "Ant Facts" to locate information and gain an overview of the contents.

Comprehension Strategy

🎯 Important Ideas

When you read you should always try to identify the important ideas of a selection. The important ideas are the essential information, facts, and details that help you understand what an author is writing about.

Ant's antennae

Ant Facts

Have you ever observed an ant crawling across a sidewalk lugging food back to its colony? To you, the food is the tiniest scrap. But to the ant, its size and weight are tremendous. Ants can carry objects that weigh several times more than they do. That is only one of the amazing facts about ants.

An ant's body is divided into three sections: the head, the thorax, and the abdomen. An ant's head is large with two antennae, which are used for smelling and feeling. Its mouth has two sets of mandibles. One set is for carrying. The other is for chewing. The thorax is the middle part of the ant. It's connected to the abdomen by a small, waistlike section. The abdomen is large and oval-shaped.

Skill Preview the title and the diagram below. Do they help you gain an idea of the article's contents?

Strategy What are some of the important ideas of this paragraph, and how do they connect to the topic of the article?

Skill How does this diagram help you locate information? What facts can you interpret from this diagram?

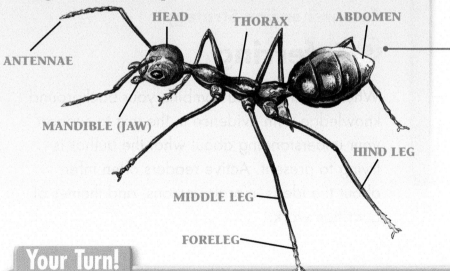

ANTENNAE · HEAD · THORAX · ABDOMEN · MANDIBLE (JAW) · HIND LEG · MIDDLE LEG · FORELEG

Your Turn!

Need a Review?
See *Envision It!* Skills and Strategies for additional help.

Ready to Try It?
Use what you've learned about graphic sources and important ideas as you read other text.

Skill

Strategy

Comprehension Skill

Graphic Sources

• Graphic sources include charts, tables, graphs, maps, illustrations, and photographs.

• They can give you an overview of a text's contents. You can also use graphics to locate information.

• Use a graphic organizer like the one below to list details about the important information you locate in the graphic sources of "Shipwreck."

Finding Shipwrecks

Detail

Detail

Detail

Comprehension Strategy

Inferring

When you infer, you combine your background knowledge with evidence in the text to support your understanding about what the author is trying to present. Active readers often infer about the ideas, morals, lessons, and themes of a written work.

New York

Queenstown

Southampton

Cherborg

41043'57" N, 49056'49" W

Shipwreck

For many years, people have spent their lives trying to find certain sunken ships. Why do they try to do this? There are several reasons.

Some people want to find shipwrecks to learn exactly what caused the ships to sink. If we find out the cause of a shipwreck, we may be able to prevent the same kind of accident from happening again.

Some scientists and explorers search for shipwrecks to learn more about the past. They want to find out how old ships were designed. They also want to see the tools people used on those ships. The study of shipwrecks is called *nautical archaeology*.

Once people find a sunken ship, they mark its location on a map. The map here shows approximately where the ocean liner *Titanic* went down. This map will help other people locate the shipwreck for years to come.

Skill How do the title and the map give you an overview of the text's contents?

Strategy What can you infer about why it is important to learn about the past? Use textual evidence to support understanding.

Skill How does the map help you understand where the *Titanic* sank?

Your Turn!

Need a Review?
See *Envision It!* Skills and Strategies for additional help.

Ready to Try It?
Use what you've learned about graphic sources and inferring as you read other text.

85

A **Day** at the **Beach**

The End

Literary Elements

Understanding a story requires knowing the four main parts of a story: character, setting, plot, and theme.

Setting - the time and place in which a story happens.

Character - a person or animal in a story.

Plot - the pattern of events in a story.

Rising Action

Climax

Conflict

Solution

Theme - the big idea of a story.

How to Identify Literary Elements

Stories are made up of the following parts: characters, setting, theme, and plot.

See It!

- Look at pages 86–87. What do they tell you about literary elements?

- Look for hints about a story's characters, setting, theme, or plot in the illustrations or other graphic elements of a text. How are the characters portrayed in the illustrations? What do the illustrations tell you about the setting, or time and place, of the story? Do the images fit with the author's descriptions?

- Visualize as you read an author's descriptions of characters and setting.

Say It!

- With a partner, read aloud the text on pages 86–87. What do you learn about characters, setting, theme, and plot? Look at the images before and after you read each description.

- Tell a partner about the theme of a story you know well. To tell about theme, think about the big idea of the story.

- Divide into groups of four. Each group member should choose a different literary element on which to focus as he or she reads an agreed-upon short story. Then each member should discuss the literary element he or she chose in relation to the story.

Do It!

- After reading, make a list of the important events that happened first, next, and last in the story. What problems do the characters encounter? How are those problems resolved? A plot usually starts with a problem and ends with a resolution, or outcome.

- Make a graphic organizer like the one below to identify the events in a story, or plot:

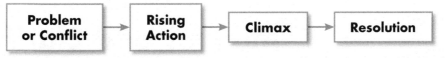

Problem or Conflict → Rising Action → Climax → Resolution

Objectives
- Explain the roles and functions of characters, including their relationships and conflicts.
- Monitor and adjust comprehension using a variety of strategies.

Envision It! | Skill Strategy

Skill

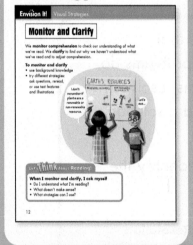

Strategy

READING STREET ONLINE
ENVISION IT! ANIMATION
www.ReadingStreet.com

Comprehension Skill

Literary Elements: Character and Plot

- Characters are the people or animals in a story.

- Plot is the pattern of events in a story. Usually, events in a plot occur in sequential order.

- A plot has a *conflict*, or problem; *rising action*, when the conflict builds; a *climax*, when characters meet the conflict; and a *resolution*, when the conflict is resolved.

- Use a graphic organizer like the one below to explain the plot in "Brave Melissa." Then explain Melissa's role and function in the plot.

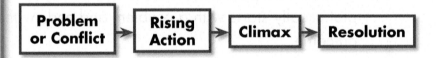

Comprehension Strategy

Monitor and Clarify

Good readers check their understanding as they read. If you don't understand something you are reading, pause. Ask yourself *What don't I understand*? Try creating a sensory image to help you understand the story. Then read on to find out what happens.

BRAVE Melissa

Most people around town knew Melissa as a sweet girl who walked her big yellow dog every day. Whether the sun was shining or freezing rain was pouring down, Melissa always walked her dog before and after school.

One winter day, the snow was coming down so fast that the sidewalk became very slippery. Melissa fell and dropped her dog's leash. The dog got confused and kept walking to the beach where he and Melissa would go during the summer. The dog was so confused that he headed toward the lake and accidentally fell through the frozen water.

By this time, Melissa and half the town were at the beach. Without hesitating, Melissa reached her hand toward the dog and pulled him from the freezing water. The dog had always seemed twice her size, but today Melissa looked like a giant. Luckily, both Melissa and the dog escaped serious harm.

Skill What is the story's conflict? How do Melissa's actions influence the story's conflict?

Strategy If you do not understand what is happening, create a sensory image from story details.

Skill What is the story's resolution? How do Melissa's actions resolve the story's conflict?

Your Turn!

 Need a Review?
See *Envision It!* Skills and Strategies for additional help.

 Ready to Try It?
Use what you've learned about literary elements and monitoring and clarifying as you read other text.

Envision It! | Skill Strategy

Skill

Strategy

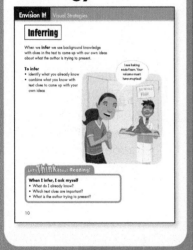

Comprehension Skill

Literary Elements: Theme and Setting

• The theme is the underlying meaning of a story.

• The theme is often not stated. You can find the theme using evidence from the story.

• The setting is where and when the story takes place. Writers use figurative language and details, such as sights and sounds, to describe the setting.

• Use a graphic organizer like the one below to describe the setting of "Alone."

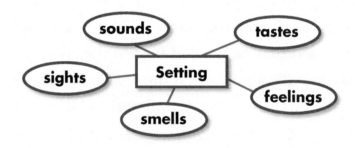

Comprehension Strategy

Inferring

When you infer, you combine your background knowledge with evidence in the text to come up with an idea about what the author is trying to present. Active readers often infer about the ideas, morals, lessons, and themes of a written work.

ALONE

Jesse heard the horses trotting and the wagon wheels creaking even after the wagon disappeared into the thick forest. Soon, those familiar sounds faded. Then he heard nothing but the summer wind rustling the tall prairie grass surrounding his family's log cabin. Jesse was all alone.

Jesse's parents had gone to town to buy supplies for the winter. They would be gone several days. His father insisted that Jesse was old enough to stay alone and manage the farm, but Jesse wasn't so sure.

Jesse milked the cow, weeded the garden, and fixed the latch on the barn door. He cooked his own potato soup and sliced some bread for dinner. That night, alone, Jesse had a hard time sleeping. Wolves howled in the distance. He was trained to use his father's musket and kept it nearby just in case. Each night, he lay in bed, nervous.

On the sixth day, Jesse heard a familiar sound. It was the wagon coming down the trail. His parents were home!

Skill After reading the title and first paragraph, which of these is the story's most likely theme?

(a) the beauty of nature
(b) love of animals
(c) surviving by yourself

Skill What figurative language does the author use in the story? Does it help you visualize the setting?

Strategy Make an inference about how Jesse is feeling at the end of the story. What evidence from the text supports this inference?

Your Turn!

Need a Review?
See *Envision It!* Skills and Strategies for additional help.

Ready to Try It?
Use what you've learned about literary elements and inferring as you read other text.

Skill

Strategy

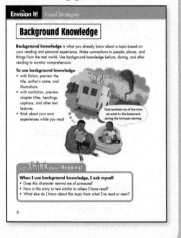

Comprehension Skill

Literary Elements: Character and Plot

- The plot is the pattern of events in a story. It includes conflict, rising action, a climax, and a resolution.

- Characters are people in a story. Characters show you their traits, or qualities, by what they say and do.

- Use a graphic organizer like the one below to help you list a character's traits. Then explain the character's role and function in the plot, relationships, and conflicts in "The Day of Two Adventures."

Comprehension Strategy

Background Knowledge

Active readers use what they already know to understand what they read. As you read, think about what you already know about people and events from your own life that are similar to those in the story.

THE DAY OF TWO ADVENTURES

Gram played tennis. She had frown lines from squinting against the sun to see the ball. Gramps's wrinkles were from smiling. "Games aren't for me," said Gramps.

Saturday morning, Gramps didn't want to climb Mt. Baldy with us.

"What a great adventure!" said Gram.

It was hard to keep up with Gram. "Gramps likes to go slow and enjoy the scenery," I panted.

"Three hours!" said Gram at the summit. Then she sat down suddenly, looking pale.

"Are you all right?" I asked.

"Climbing used up my energy, but lunch will fix that." Gram opened her pack. "Oh, no! I left our lunch at home."

I looked down the trail and saw Gramps approaching. "When did you leave home?" I asked when he arrived.

"Right after you," said Gramps. "I saw your lunch."

"What's that smell?"

"I decided to have my own adventure." Gramps took some muffins out of his pack. "I had never baked before, so I tried baking muffins."

Skill How does the relationship between Gram and Gramps contribute to the story's plot?

Skill Explain how Gram's character traits contribute to the conflict in this story.

Strategy Do you know someone like Gram? How does having this knowledge help you understand her character?

Your Turn!

⏸ Need a Review?
See *Envision It!* Skills and Strategies for additional help.

▶ Ready to Try It?
Use what you've learned about literary elements and background knowledge as you read other text.

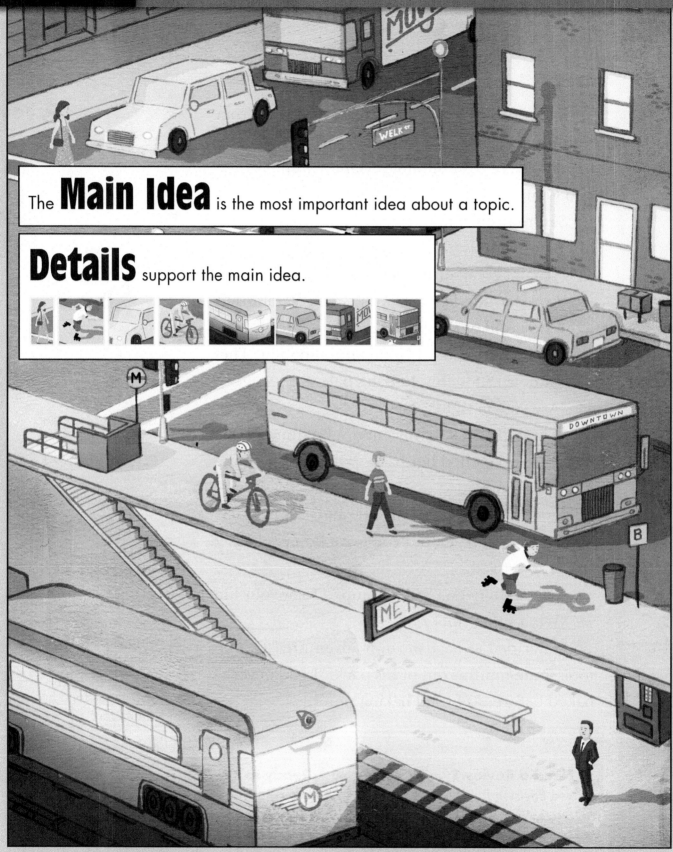

The **Main Idea** is the most important idea about a topic.

Details support the main idea.

How to Identify Main Idea and Details

The main idea is the most important idea. Details are pieces of information that tell more about—or help explain—this main idea.

See It!

- Look at page 96. What details are pictured? What do you think is the main idea? Why? How do the details of the picture help you understand this main idea? Explain.

- Look for a sentence or sentences where the author tells what the selection will be about or what the author wants to prove or show through writing.

Say It!

- With a partner, state the main idea of your reading. Come up with at least one example from the reading that supports the statement. If you can't do this, you may have not correctly identified the main idea.

- To check if you have correctly identified the main idea, tell it to a partner after reading. Ask him or her: "Does my main idea make sense? Does it cover all the important details?"

Do It!

- Use a web like the one below to identify main idea and details. What is the story about? What details help support this main idea?

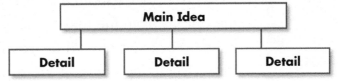

- Write a paragraph explaining why a book or film is your favorite. Afterward, circle the main idea and underline details that tell more about it. Do your details support the main idea?

Envision It! Skill Strategy

Skill

Strategy

Comprehension Skill

Main Idea and Details

• The main idea is the most important idea about a topic. Details are small pieces of information that tell more about the main idea.

• Sometimes the author states the main idea of a paragraph or an entire article in a single sentence at the beginning, middle, or end.

• Use a graphic organizer like the one below to help you summarize and maintain the meanings of main ideas and supporting details from "Bronze." Be sure to keep the ideas and details in logical order.

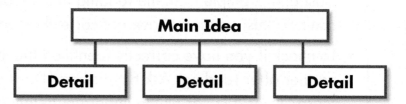

Comprehension Strategy

Visualize

Active readers visualize as they read. They use the details from the text to make pictures in their minds. For example, when you read nonfiction text, visualizing some of the supporting details can help you understand information. As you read, evaluate the impact the sensory details and imagery have on the story.

Bronze

People have used bronze for thousands of years to make many things. Bronze is a soft metal made from copper and tin. It cannot be hammered or bent, so it is not a good material for making tools. However, in molten or liquid form, it can be shaped into things such as statues, pots, and bowls.

Skill What is the main idea of this paragraph?

Thousands of years ago, bronze was shaped using the "lost-wax method." In this method, a model was made using plaster or clay. Then it was coated in wax followed by another layer of plaster or clay. When heated, the wax melted away, leaving a space. The bronze was melted and poured into the space. When the bronze cooled, the plaster or clay was taken off. Using this method, only one item could be made from the model.

Strategy As you read the details in this paragraph, what pictures or images do you visualize? How does this help you understand the information presented?

In time, molds were formed out of other materials, such as wood. A wooden mold could be used again and again. It was pressed into sand, and when it was removed, the impression was left in the sand. Bronze was poured into the sand. Later, the bronze was removed, and the surface was smoothed.

Skill Write the main idea of this paragraph in your own words.

Bronze is still used today. You may even have some items made from bronze in your home!

Your Turn!

 Need a Review?
See *Envision It!* Skills and Strategies for additional help.

Ready to Try It?
Use what you've learned about main idea and details and visualizing as you read other text.

Envision It! | Skill Strategy

Skill

Strategy

Comprehension Skill

🎯 Main Idea and Details

- The main idea is the most important idea about a topic.

- Sometimes the author tells you the main idea. Sometimes you must figure it out for yourself.

- Supporting details tell more about the main idea.

- Use a graphic organizer like the one below to help you summarize the main idea and details from "Aretha: An American Queen." Maintain the meaning of the ideas and details, and place them in logical order.

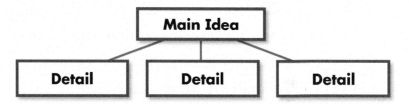

Comprehension Strategy

🎯 Text Structure

Text structure is the way a selection is organized. A selection may describe events in a sequence, or in a cause-and-effect pattern. It may also use a series of main ideas and details. Active readers use text structure to help them understand what a selection is about.

Aretha
An American Queen

The United States is not ruled by a queen. There is a queen who rules in the hearts of American music lovers, though. That queen is Aretha Franklin.

Aretha Franklin was born in Memphis, Tennessee, in 1942. Both her parents were religious gospel music singers. Aretha grew up listening to gospel music. She also learned to sing it as a child.

Even when she was little, people saw that she was a talented singer. Aretha began singing on stage in her early teens. She sang with her father. Her first album, *The Gospel Sound of Aretha Franklin,* was released in 1956. She was only 14!

When Aretha turned 18, she moved to New York. Eventually, she developed her own style of singing. It came from deep inside her. It was a mixture of gospel and rhythm and blues. This music was called "soul music." Aretha sang it so well that she became known as "The Queen of Soul."

Aretha was voted into the Rock and Roll Hall of Fame in 1987. Her songs are still played on the radio today. For many people, she still rules as queen.

Skill In your own words, what is the main idea of this paragraph?

Skill What is the main idea of this paragraph? Give one detail that supports the main idea.

Strategy Explain how the sequential pattern in this text helped you understand what you read.

Your Turn!

⏸ Need a Review?
See *Envision It!* Skills and Strategies for additional help.

▶ Ready to Try It?
Use what you've learned about main idea and details and text structure as you read other text.

Objectives

● Summarize the main ideas and supporting details in a text. ● Analyze how the organization of a text affects the way ideas are related.

Skill

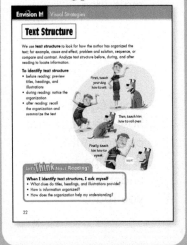

Strategy

Comprehension Skill

Main Idea and Details

- The main idea of a selection is the most important idea about the selection's topic.

- The author may state the main idea in a single sentence. Sometimes the reader must figure it out on his or her own.

- Use a graphic organizer like the one below to summarize the main idea and details in "Works of Art or Works of Aliens?" Be sure to summarize while maintaining meaning, and organize your summary in logical order.

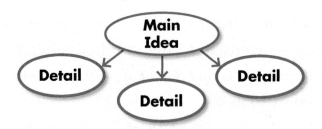

Comprehension Strategy

Text Structure

Text structure is the organizational pattern of a text. The piece may show relationships among ideas in sequence, in cause-and-effect patterns, or in a series of comparisons and contrasts. Active readers analyze how text structure influences relationships among ideas.

Works of ART or Works of ALIENS?

In the farm fields of Southern England during the 1970s, simple designs, called crop circles, were formed from flattened stalks of grain. Some were only a few feet in diameter. Others were as big as 1,500 feet across. How did they get there?

Some scientists claimed these mysterious designs were caused by the weather. Other people believed they were caused by aliens or by humans here on Earth. No one knew for sure. More designs appeared in fields each year.

In 1991, two men calling themselves crop artists admitted they were responsible for some of the crop circles. Crop artists think of their designs as art. Each one takes up to two weeks to finish, but crop artists hardly ever take credit for their designs. They believe that the mystery is part of their art.

The relationship between crop artists and farmers sometimes benefits both parties. While farmers provide the "canvas," the artists bring in the tourists. Farmers often charge tourists a small fee to see the circles. Are farmers concerned about the origin of the crop circles? Many feel that as long as they are well made, people can believe whatever they want to believe.

Strategy After reading the first paragraph, can you tell how ideas will be organized in this text?

Skill Summarize the main ideas and details in what you've read so far.

Skill What is the main idea of this selection?
a) causes of crop circles
b) aliens from outer space
c) tourism in England

Your Turn!

 Need a Review?
See *Envision It!* Skills and Strategies for additional help.

 Ready to Try It?
Use what you've learned about main idea and details and text structure as you read other text.

103

Sequence

Sequence refers to the order of events in a text.
We use sequence when we list the steps in a process.

How to Identify Sequence

The sequence is the order in which events take place, from first to last.

See It!

- As you read, notice whether the story has illustrations or other images. If so, do they give you any clues about what happens first, next, and last? Use pictures to help you understand sequence.

- Look at page 104. What do you see happening first, next, and last? Tell the sequence to a partner.

- Look for clue words, such as *first, next, then,* or *after.* They will help tell you the order of events.

Say It!

- Take turns telling a partner what happens first, next, and last in a selection.

- Some authors tell a story out of sequence. With a partner, paraphrase, or tell in your own words, what happens in a story in time order. How does this help you understand the events of the story?

Do It!

- Draw images of a story's events on a sheet of paper or a computer program. Be sure to put your illustrations in order of first, next, and last to identify sequence.

- Make a sequence diagram or a time line, such as the one below, to help you keep track of the most important events in a story.

Skill

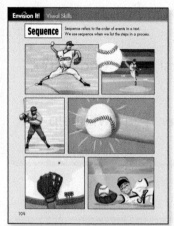

Strategy

Comprehension Skill

Sequence

- The sequence of events is the order in which events take place, from first to last.

- Clue words such as *first, next, then,* and *finally* may show sequence. Other clues are dates and the times of day.

- *While* and *at the same time* are clues that events are occurring at once.

- Use a graphic organizer like the one below to put the events in "A Flag Unfurled" in sequence. Then write a summary of the events in sequence.

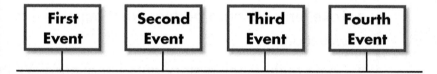

| First Event | Second Event | Third Event | Fourth Event |

Comprehension Strategy

Inferring

When you infer, you combine your own knowledge with evidence in the text to come up with an idea about what the author is presenting. Active readers often infer about the ideas, morals, and themes of a written work.

106

A Flag Unfurled

Do you know how many times the American flag has changed? From 1777 to 1960 Congress has changed the flag more than a dozen times!

In 1776, George Washington needed a symbol for the country. Washington had used the Grand Union flag during the Revolutionary War. The Grand Union flag had the British Union Jack in the upper left corner. In 1777, the Continental Congress passed the first Flag Act. The Act stated that the flag be made of 13 stripes and 13 stars.

Strategy What inference can you make about the Grand Union flag? Why was it unsuitable for the new Union?

One year earlier, Betsy Ross, a seamstress from Philadelphia, reported that she had sewed the first American flag. As the legend goes, Washington had visited her shop and showed her a flag design. The result was the first "stars and stripes" flag. It had a circle of 13 stars that represented the original 13 colonies.

The "stars and stripes" flag remained in use for several years. Then, in 1791, Vermont was added to the Union. Another star and stripe were added. After that, another star and stripe were added for every new state, until finally, in 1818, Congress decided to keep the number of stripes at 13, and allow the addition of a new star for each new state.

Skill What clue word tells you that the practice of adding stripes to the flag stopped?

Skill What is the earliest event that appears in this article?

Your Turn!

 Need a Review?
See *Envision It!* Skills and Strategies for additional help.

 Ready to Try It?
Use what you've learned about sequence and inferring as you read other text.

Objectives

• Summarize and paraphrase information in a text. • Analyze how the organization of a text affects the way ideas are related.

Envision It! | Skill Strategy

Skill

Strategy

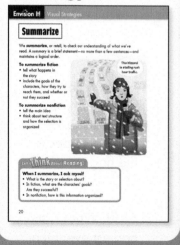

READING STREET ONLINE
ENVISION IT! ANIMATIONS
www.ReadingStreet.com

Comprehension Skill

🎯 Sequence

• The sequence of events is the order in which they take place, from first to last.

• Clue words such as *first*, *next*, and *then* may show sequence in a story or an article, but not always. Other clues are dates and times.

• Two events can happen at the same time. *While* and *at the same time* are clue words.

• Use a graphic organizer like the one below to chart the sequence of events in "Kid Inventor." Then think about how the sequence influences the relationships among ideas in the text.

First Event	Second Event	Third Event	Fourth Event

Comprehension Strategy

🎯 Summarize

Active readers summarize to check their understanding of a selection. As you read "Kid Inventor," summarize by stating main ideas that maintain meaning and leaving out unimportant details. Summarizing helps you make sure you understand and remember what you read. A good summary should be brief and use a reader's own words.

Kid Inventor

Some of the most amazing inventions have not come from expensive laboratories. They have come from children your age!

Strategy What are one or two of the main ideas of this article that you could use in a summary?

One of the most delicious inventions in the world came from an eleven-year-old named Frank Epperson, who in 1905 created the frozen fruit bar. First, Epperson made a fruit drink for himself. Instead of finishing it, he left his drink outside overnight with a stick in it. Then, temperatures in San Francisco dropped to below freezing, and the drink froze. The next morning he discovered that he liked the taste of the frozen fruit drink.

Skill What is the last thing that Epperson did with his invention?

Epperson couldn't apply for a patent to claim ownership of the invention until much later, because at the time he was too young. He waited many years, until he was an adult, to patent the treat. Later, Epperson sold the idea to a company, which then produced the treats that you find in the store today.

Skill Which words in this paragraph tell you about the sequence of events?

Your Turn!

❚❚ Need a Review?
See *Envision It!* Skills and Strategies for additional help.

▷ Ready to Try It?
Use what you've learned about sequence and summarizing as you read other text.

Objectives
- Summarize and paraphrase information in a text.

Skill

Strategy

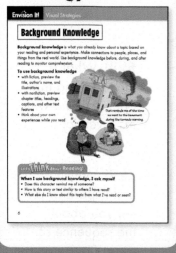

Comprehension Skill

Sequence

- Sequence is the order of events in a selection. Dates and times of day or clue words such as *first, next,* and *then* can help you summarize the sequence of events in a text or story.

- Clue words such as *meanwhile* or *during* signal events happening at the same time.

- Use a graphic organizer like the one below to summarize the sequence of events in "What Do You Know About Harlem?"

First Event	Second Event	Third Event	Fourth Event

Comprehension Strategy

Background Knowledge

Background knowledge is what you can find out or what you already know about a topic. Active readers connect their background knowledge to the text to help them understand it. They add to and revise their background knowledge as they read and think about the text.

WHAT DO YOU KNOW ABOUT HARLEM?

Harlem was founded in 1658 as a Dutch settlement, and through the 1700s it was a farming area. Later, high-class houses and apartments were built there, but the hard times of the panic of 1893 left many of these places empty. Many African Americans had moved to the north to find jobs. Some settled in Harlem. Before World War I, Harlem became the largest African American neighborhood in the United States.

Skill As you read, what clues help you summarize the sequence of events in the selection?

In the 1920s, music, literature, and arts began to blossom in a time known as the Harlem Renaissance. Harlem offered amazing music in the form of jazz, blues, and ragtime. Shows at the Apollo Theatre and the Cotton Club helped race relations in America.

Strategy How does your background knowledge about American history help you understand this paragraph?

The books, poems, and art showed a strong sense of pride. This was the first time that African American arts gained attention from the whole country. The Great Depression brought an end to the Harlem Renaissance, but not before America had been changed forever.

Skill Do you need the actual dates to summarize the text's sequence? Why or why not?

Your Turn!

Need a Review?
See *Envision It!* Skills and Strategies for additional help.

Ready to Try It?
Use what you've learned about sequence and background knowledge as you read other text.

Author's Viewpoint/Bias

An author's viewpoint is the way that an author looks at the subject or ideas he or she is writing about.

Bias in writing shows strong feelings for or against something.

How to Understand Author's Viewpoint and Bias

An author's viewpoint refers to the way an author approaches the topic that he or she is writing about. Bias in writing shows strong feelings for or against something.

See It!

- Look for clue words in a text that signal an author's bias, such as *should, better, favorite,* or *great.*

- Usually editorials and letters to the editor in a newspaper have a bias, whereas straight news stories are unbiased and report both sides of an issue. Find a newspaper and examine an article for bias and viewpoint.

Say It!

- Talk with a partner about things you've read or seen that show an author's bias. Examples could be television commercials, essays, and political speeches.

- What is your favorite snack? Tell a partner why this snack is the best snack to eat. You will be showing bias toward this snack from your viewpoint as a snack eater.

Do It!

- Make a graphic organizer like the one below to help you figure out an author's viewpoint or bias. After filling out your chart, can you tell what the author's viewpoint or biases are?

Statement of opinion	Support	Opposing argument

- Write a profile for yourself. This should include where you're from, your interests, and so on. How do these things affect your viewpoint?

Classify and Categorize

When we classify and categorize, we look at how things are related based on their characteristics.

114

How to Classify and Categorize

When we classify and categorize, we look at how people or things are related based on their characteristics. You can sort things into groups based on shape, size, color, and so on.

See It!

- Look at page 114. What do you see? How does the picture help you understand classifying and categorizing?

- Look at items around the classroom. What things are related to each other? With a partner, make a list of the things you see that you can put into groups.

Say It!

- Picture a place you have been before, such as a park, grocery store, or school. With a partner, name things that you see there. For example, you might see apples, bananas, milk, and juice at a grocery store. Take turns naming items and placing them into groups.

Do It!

- Make a graphic organizer like the one below. Use it to help you classify and categorize information on a topic:

Mammals	Reptiles
dogs, bears, zebras, raccoons	lizards, snakes, turtles, crocodiles

- Challenge yourself to look for things at home that you can classify and categorize. For example, you can categorize items from a cookbook recipe. Group together spices, wet or dry ingredients, and so on.

WORDS! Vocabulary

Related Words

Context Clues

Antonyms

Synonyms

Prefixes

Suffixes

Dictionary

Thesaurus

Multiple-Meaning Words

Base Words/Root Words

Word Origins: Roots

116

Vocabulary Skills and Strategies

As you read,
- look for prefixes, suffixes, or other word parts.
- look for words in the surrounding text to figure out word meaning.
- use a dictionary, a glossary, or a thesaurus to find definitions.

Vocabulary skills and strategies are tools you use to help you figure out the meanings of words. This will help you better understand what you read.

Ready to Try It? ▶

Related Words

Related words are words that all have the same base word.

Illustrate

Reillustrate

Illustrator

Strategy for Related Words

1. Find the base word in your unknown word.
2. Identify the meaning of the base word.
3. Guess the meaning of the unfamiliar word. Does it make sense in the sentence?
4. Use a dictionary to check your guess.

Context Clues

Context clues are the words and sentences found around an unknown word that may help you figure out a word's meaning.

I saw many animals at the zoo! I saw an *elephant*, a *lion*, *capybaras*, and a *monkey*.

Strategy for Context Clues

1. Look for clues in the words and phrases around the unknown word.
2. Take a guess at the word's meaning. Does it make sense in the sentence?
3. Use a dictionary to check your guess.

119

driftwood

hammocks

tweezers

algae

concealed

lamented

sea urchins

sternly

Vocabulary Strategy for

Unfamiliar Words

Context Clues As you read, you may see a word you don't know. Often you can use context to determine the meaning of a new word. *Context* means "the words and sentences near an unfamiliar word or words."

1. Reread the sentence with the unfamiliar word. The author may include a synonym or other context clue to the word's meaning.

2. If you need help, read the surrounding sentences for context clues.

3. Think about the clues and then decide on the meaning of the word.

4. Check to see that this meaning makes sense in the sentence.

Read "My Special Island" on page 121. Use context clues to help you determine the meanings of unfamiliar words.

Words to Write Reread "My Special Island." Imagine you are at the beach. Write a paragraph about what you see, hear, taste, smell, and touch. Use words from the *Words to Know* list.

My Special Island

I like to daydream about my special island. It has the most beautiful beach for exploring. I walk along the sand and admire the wild driftwood shapes, polished by the waves and sun. I pause beside a tidal pool and watch crabs, sea urchins, and other strange animals.

Standing in the water, I look at a forest of algae stretching as far as I can see. I wonder what strange and beautiful creatures lie concealed in that underwater forest. In my dream I am a world-famous scientist. Armed with my microscope, tweezers, and diving equipment, I learn all the secrets of the ocean world.

After a long day of amazing discoveries, I head for one of the hammocks under the palm trees. There I store my treasures and lie down, letting a gentle breeze rock me to sleep.

"Martin!" Ms. Smith says sternly. "Wake up and get to work!" Oh, well. Back to arithmetic. I have often lamented my bad habit of daydreaming during classes.

Your Turn!

Need a Review?
For additional help with using context clues, see page 119.

Ready to Try It?
As you read other text, use context clues to help you determine the meanings of unfamiliar words.

hogan

mesa

turquoise

bandana
bracelet
jostled
Navajo

Vocabulary Strategy for

Unfamiliar Words

Context Clues As you read, you may see a word you do not know. Often the author will give clues to determine and clarify the meaning of an unfamiliar word. Check the context—the words and sentences around the unfamiliar word—for these clues.

1. Reread the sentence where the unfamiliar word appears.

2. Is there a specific clue to the word's meaning?

3. For more help, read the sentences around the sentence with the unfamiliar word. Look for words or phrases that suggest a reasonable meaning.

4. Try the meaning in the sentence with the unfamiliar word. Does it make sense?

Read "At the Navajo Nation Fair" on page 123. Use context clues to help you figure out the meanings of the *Words to Know*.

Words to Write Reread "At the Navajo Nation Fair." Imagine that you are writing an advertisement for things you can do and buy at the fair. Use words from the *Words to Know* in your advertisement.

At the Navajo Nation Fair

"I'm too old to go to the fair," I told my granddaughter, Yolanda.

"Aw, come on, Ami," Yolanda said. "Rikki and I really want to go, and Mami is too busy with the horses to come."

Yolanda looked up at me, smiling hopefully over the red bandana she wore as a scarf around her neck. How could I say no?

I had not left the hogan where I lived for quite some time. I spent many days there working diligently to make woven rugs to sell at the fair. I was going to give them to my son, Ed, to take, but he was taking care of his ill wife.

The trip to the fair was a long, bumpy ride across the desert floor and past several large mesas. When we got to the fairground gate, Yolanda and Rikki jumped out and disappeared with cries of "Thank you, Ami!" hanging in the air.

The hordes of people at the Navajo fair bumped and jostled me. To get out of the way, I walked over to a booth selling jewelry with inlaid turquoise stones. I started to slip a bracelet over my wrist, but what really caught my eye was a lovely silver necklace. Suddenly Yolanda appeared at my side.

"Don't buy it, Ami!" she said. "Rikki and I bought you a present for bringing us to the fair." And there in the palm of her hand was the necklace's twin. "Let's go see the rest of the fair together, Ami," Yolanda said happily.

Your Turn!

 Need a Review?
For additional help using context clues, see page 119.

 Ready to Try It?
As you read other text, use context clues to help you determine the meanings of unfamiliar words.

Objectives
• Determine the meanings of unfamiliar words or multiple-meaning words by using the context of the sentence.

Envision It! | **Words to Know**

Dalmatian

frilly

promenading

sprained

substitute

Vocabulary Strategy for

Unfamiliar Words

Context Clues As you read, you will find unfamiliar words. See if you can use context clues to figure out the meaning of a new word. *Context* means "the words and sentences near an unfamiliar word or words."

1. Read the words and sentences around the unfamiliar word. Are there clues that help you determine the meaning of the unfamiliar word?

2. To help find context clues, you can look for a word or words set off by commas. Also look for examples, comparisons, or contrasts that suggest the meaning of the word.

3. Put the clues together and decide what you think the word means.

4. If you cannot find the meaning quickly, look up the word in a dictionary.

Read "Dogs on Parade" on page 125. Look for context clues that help you determine and clarify the meanings of unfamiliar words.

Words to Write Reread "Dogs on Parade." Imagine that you are writing an entry in your journal about the dog show. Use words from the *Words to Know* list in your journal entry.

Dogs on Parade

"Hello, everyone, and welcome to the third annual Westown Dog Show. I'm your radio host, Spot the Dalmatian. As you might guess, I got my name because I'm a white dog covered with black spots. And I usually compete in the dog show. But just last week I jumped down from a couch and injured my leg. The vet says I sprained it. Maybe that's why my owners tell me to stay off of the furniture. Anyway, I'm here today to bring you all of the action from the show.

"And here we go! The dogs have entered the building and are all walking in a line around the arena. I wish you could see them promenading around this big hall. They all look great!

"The first dog is my friend Dot. She's walking for me. Because of my leg, I needed a substitute, or someone to take my place, while my leg heals. And right behind her is Sandy the cocker spaniel. She looks so pretty with that frilly collar she wears. Just a piece of lacy white cloth can work wonders!

"Well, it's time to break for a commercial. Stay tuned, and I'll be back with you in sixty seconds!"

Your Turn!

 Need a Review?
For additional help with using context clues, see page 119.

 Ready to Try It?
As you read other text, use context clues to help you determine the meanings of unfamiliar words.

Envision It! | **Words to Know**

cavities

episode

strict

combination

demonstrates

profile

Vocabulary Strategy for

⟳ Unfamiliar Words

Context Clues You may come across an unfamiliar word in your reading. You can use the context, or the words and sentences around the word, to help you determine and clarify the meaning of a word.

1. Reread the sentence in which the unfamiliar word appears. Try creating an analogy with the unfamiliar word and a possible synonym you know.

2. If not, read the surrounding sentences for context clues.

3. Put the clues together and decide what you think the word means.

4. Try the meaning in the sentence. Does it make sense?

Read "Trouble in TV Land" on page 127. Look for context clues that help you determine and clarify the meanings of unfamiliar words.

Words to Write Reread "Trouble in TV Land." Write a letter to your favorite fictional television character about the way he or she solves a problem. State your opinions and give reasons to support them. Use words in the *Words to Know* list.

Trouble in TV Land

Can a TV show teach us how to win friends in the real world? Most sitcoms solve problems in thirty minutes flat, minus about eight minutes of commercials. They present an extremely simple and reassuring view of the world. A single episode demonstrates how to teach a bully the value of kindness, or how to overcome your worst fears. Nice-looking young people have a high profile in these shows, and they almost always solve their problems by the end. Plus, the commercials tell you things such as how to prevent cavities and whiten your teeth. These commercial messages claim they can save you from tooth decay and so much more. If you will only buy the right clothes and choose the right cell phone, everyone will love you and you will be happy.

In the real world, problems aren't so easily solved. Things you don't enjoy, such as having a strict teacher or parent, may actually be good for you. Everyone has problems. Some are as simple as forgetting a locker combination, but others are tough. You can't just make a wish and watch a failing grade go away, for example. To solve problems in the real world, you must be honest and willing to try hard, sometimes for a long time.

Your Turn!

⏸ Need a Review?
For additional help with using context clues, see page 119.

▶ Ready to Try It?
As you read other text, use context clues to help you figure out the meanings of unfamiliar words.

Envision It! | Words to Know

armor

plunged

serpent

encases

extinct

hideous

Vocabulary Strategy for
↻ Unfamiliar Words

Context Clues As you read, you may come to a word you do not know. Look for clues in the context—the words and sentences around the word—to help you determine the meaning of the unfamiliar word.

1. Reread the sentence in which the unfamiliar word appears. Does the author include a synonym, an antonym, or other clue to the word's meaning?

2. If you need more help, read the sentences around the unfamiliar word.

3. Put the clues together and think of a logical meaning for the word. Does this meaning make sense in the sentence?

Read "The Land of Imagination" on page 129. Use context clues to help you determine and clarify the meanings of any unfamiliar words.

Words to Write Reread "The Land of Imagination." Write a description of the dinosaur you know the most about. Use words from the *Words to Know* list in your description.

The Land of Imagination

Dinosaurs are extinct creatures that used to roam the Earth. We can only imagine how the Earth quaked beneath the weight of these vanished creatures. Still, we have no trouble imagining them eating, drinking, or fighting with one another.

A beast like a serpent with legs, only many times larger, stands in the shallows of a warm ocean eating immense, strange water plants. On the shore, a hideous lizard with teeth like deadly knives stands on its powerful haunches. It roars as it charges the plant-eater. Soon both are plunged beneath the water, locked in a giant struggle. When they surface, the dying plant-eater's tormented cries echo through the trees.

Another dinosaur draws near. A thick, hornlike armor encases its thick body and long tail. These plates cover every square inch that the terrible lizard might attack. Angry-looking spikes bristle from the dinosaur's back as well. The dinosaur waits to see if any dinner will be left for it. Did it really happen like this? We will never know for sure, but in the land of our imagination, it did.

Your Turn!

 Need a Review?

For additional help with using context clues, see page 119.

 Ready to Try It?

As you read other text, use context clues to help you figure out the meanings of unfamiliar words.

Envision It! | Words to Know

cruised

hydrogen

explosion

drenching

era

criticizing

Vocabulary Strategy for

🎯 Unfamiliar Words

Context Clues As you read, you may see a word you do not know. Often the author will give clues to determine and clarify the meaning of an unfamiliar word. Check the words and sentences around the unfamiliar word for these clues.

1. Reread the sentence where the unfamiliar word appears.

2. Is there a specific clue to the word's meaning?

3. For more help, read the sentences around the sentence with the unfamiliar word.

4. Try the clue's meaning in the sentence with the unfamiliar word. Does it make sense?

Read "The Birth of the Automobile" on page 131. Use the context to help you determine and clarify the meanings of the *Words to Know*.

Words to Write Reread "The Birth of the Automobile." Imagine you live in that era. Write about the transportation you are using. Use words from the *Words to Know* list in your writing.

The Birth
of the Automobile

The automobile may well have been the most important invention in transportation history. However, it took many people many years to come up with an engine that worked well. In 1771 a Frenchman invented a three-wheeled sort of tractor. It ran on steam power, and it cruised along at 2½ miles per hour. (Get a horse!) It crashed into a stone wall. Don't worry—all the riders survived! In 1807 a Swiss man invented an engine that used a mix of hydrogen and oxygen for fuel. (Can you imagine the explosion?) Neither of these succeeded.

Not until the 1880s did inventors come up with an engine that was practical. A gas engine was mounted on an open coach. (If it rained, the driver and guests got a drenching!) This four-wheeled vehicle had a top speed of 10 miles per hour.

Improvements happened fast after that. The era of the automobile had begun. This age has continued to the present time and shows no signs of stopping. Instead of criticizing the early cars, we should admire them for pointing the way.

Your Turn!

** Need a Review?**
For additional help with using context clues, see page 119.

▷ Ready to Try It?
As you read other text, use context clues to help you determine the meanings of unfamiliar words.

Antonyms

An antonym is a word that has the opposite meaning of another word. *Day* is an antonym for *night*.

Smooth

Bumpy

Antonym = Opposite

Strategy for Antonyms

1. Identify the word for which you want to find an antonym.
2. Think of other words or phrases that have the opposite meaning.
3. Use a thesaurus to help you find antonyms.
4. Use a dictionary to check antonyms' meanings so that you use the word that best communicates your ideas.

Synonyms

Synonyms are two or more words that have the same meaning or nearly the same meaning.

Wash

Synonym = Same

Clean

Strategy for Synonyms

1. Identify the word for which you want to find a synonym.
2. Think of other words or phrases that have the same, or almost the same, meaning.
3. Use a thesaurus to help you find more synonyms, and make a list.
4. Use a dictionary to find the word that best communicates your ideas.

133

Envision It! | Words to Know

confidence

outfield

windup

fastball

mocking

unique

weakness

READING STREET ONLINE
VOCABULARY ACTIVITIES
www.ReadingStreet.com

Vocabulary Strategy for

Antonyms

Context Clues Antonyms are words with opposite meanings. You can use analogies, or comparisons that show relationships, to help you understand antonyms. For example, *cold* is to *hot* as *few* is to *many*. Sometimes an author writes an antonym near a word to help readers understand the word.

1. Use what you know about antonyms to complete this analogy: *weakness* is to *strength* as *illness* is to _____.

2. When you read a word you don't know, reread the sentence with the unfamiliar word. Look for an antonym or context clues.

3. If you find an antonym, try using it in place of the unfamiliar word. Does it make sense?

Read "Play Ball!" on page 135. Look for nearby antonyms to help you determine or clarify the meanings of the *Words to Know*.

Words to Write Reread "Play Ball!" Write a paragraph about a baseball game you've seen. Use words from the *Words to Know* list in your writing.

Play Ball!

Many young people dream of becoming a great baseball player. Only a few will be able to do this. One reason is that you must first have a lot of talent. Another is that you must be willing to work very hard. With work comes skill. With skill comes the confidence a great player needs.

For a pitcher, every windup and throw of the ball helps him or her learn something. Whether learning to deliver a smoking fastball or a dancing curve, the pitcher must master difficult moves. A hitter learns with every at-bat which pitch should go by and which should be slammed into the outfield. Even the mocking "Heybatterbatterbatter" of the other team can help build a hitter's concentration.

Being dedicated, the great player of tomorrow is willing to work on a weakness until it finally becomes a strength. The really great player is unique. He or she has passed the common level of play expected and has invented a style that stands out. Every player who tries hard and loves the game, though, is a winner, no matter what.

Your Turn!

 Need a Review?
For additional help with antonyms, see page 132.

 Ready to Try It?
As you read other text, use what you've learned about antonyms to help you understand it.

- Determine the meanings of unfamiliar words or multiple-meaning words by using the context of the sentence.

Envision It! Words to Know

choir

barber

teenager

appreciate
released
religious
slavery

READING STREET ONLINE
VOCABULARY ACTIVITIES
www.ReadingStreet.com

Vocabulary Strategy for

Antonyms

Context Clues Antonyms are words that have the opposite meaning of other words. For example, *fast* is an antonym for *slow.* Using context clues, or nearby words and sentences, can help you determine the meaning of an antonym.

1. When you see an unfamiliar word, reread the context around the word.

2. Look for an antonym that shows a contrast with the unfamiliar word.

3. Give the unfamiliar word the opposite meaning of the antonym. Does this meaning make sense in the sentence?

Read "Out of Great Pain, Great Music." Check the context of words you don't know. Look for antonyms to help you determine and clarify the meanings of unfamiliar words.

Words to Write Reread "Out of Great Pain, Great Music." Write a paragraph about what you know about blues music. Use words from the *Words to Know* list in your writing.

Out of Great Pain, GREAT MUSIC

It is hard to understand how people in the United States ever put up with slavery, since Americans value freedom so highly. However, for some 250 years, African Americans were held as slaves. Every child of a slave, from infant to teenager, also became the owner's property. Slaves performed many jobs, from cook to field hand to barber.

Slavery caused great sorrow and pain, but it also gave rise to some of the world's most moving music. Spirituals are religious folk songs that began among slaves. They would sing these songs to help raise their spirits. Church gave them a place to express their hope for a better life to come. The choir made powerful music about that hope.

Slavery ended for African Americans some 140 years ago. But spirituals remain an important part of life for many African Americans today. People of many races and backgrounds have come to appreciate spirituals. Many people also love blues music, which also originated from the African American experience of slavery. Many African American singers have released recordings of blues music and spirituals that have sold millions of copies all around the world.

Your Turn!

 Need a Review?
For additional help with antonyms, see page 132.

 Ready to Try It?
As you read other text, use what you've learned about antonyms to help you understand it.

137

Objectives

- Determine the meanings of synonyms by using the context of the sentence. • Write analogies with synonyms you know. • Use a dictionary, a glossary, or a thesaurus to locate information about words.

Envision It! | Words to Know

sterile

specialize

scarce

critical

enables

mucus

Vocabulary Strategy for

◎ Synonyms

Context Clues Synonyms are different words that mean almost the same thing. For example, *cold* is to *freezing* as *hot* is to *boiling*. The words *cold* and *freezing* are synonyms. *Hot* and *boiling* are also synonyms. Complete this analogy: *scarce* is to *rare* as *expensive* is to _____.

1. Read the words and sentences around an unfamiliar word. Is there a synonym you know nearby?

2. Use the known synonym in place of the unfamiliar word. Does the synonym help you determine or clarify the word's meaning?

3. If you need help, look up the word in a printed or electronic thesaurus. A thesaurus is a book that contains synonyms of words.

Read "Small but Mighty" on page 139. Check the context clues or nearby synonyms to determine or clarify the meanings of words.

Words to Write Reread "Small but Mighty." List some of the characteristics of bacteria and how bacteria can adapt. Use words from the *Words to Know* list in your writing and a thesaurus to find alternate word choices to make your writing lively.

Small but MIGHTY

Bacteria are made up of just one cell. However, they adapt just like all living things. In fact, their small size enables them to adapt quickly. We have medicines to kill harmful bacteria. However, bacteria have changed so that they can stand up to many medicines. Medicines that still work against them are becoming scarce, or rare. Doctors use these medicines less often so bacteria will not "learn" how to live with them.

Different bacteria specialize in different ways. Some live in your gut and help you digest food. Others are critical, or important, to the making of soil. They break down dead plant and animal matter.

Most bacteria are helpful, but a few can harm us. One kind causes a disease called pneumonia. The bacteria reproduce quickly inside the body. They give off poisons. The body fights back. It raises its temperature. It produces more mucus to protect the lining of organs.

It is best to keep surfaces as sterile as possible so you do not touch harmful bacteria.

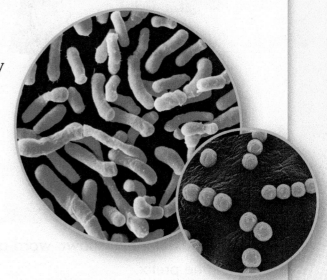

Your Turn!

 Need a Review?
For additional help with synonyms, see page 133.

 Ready to Try It?
As you read other text, use what you've learned about synonyms to help you understand it.

Prefixes

A prefix is a word part added onto the front of a base word to form a new word.

Formal

Informal

Strategy for Prefixes

1. Look at the unknown word and identify the prefix.
2. What does the base word mean? If you're not sure, check the dictionary.
3. Use what you know about the base word and the prefix to figure out the meaning of the unknown word.
4. Use the dictionary to check your guess.

Common Prefixes and Their Meanings

un-	not
re-	again, back
in-	not
dis-	not, opposite of
pre-	before

Suffixes

A suffix is a word part added to the end of a base word to form a new word.

Sleeve

Sleeveless

Common Suffixes and Their Meanings

Suffix	Meaning
-ly	characteristic of
-tion	act, process
-able	can be done
-ment	action or process
-less	without

Strategy for Suffixes

1. Look at the unknown word and identify the suffix.
2. What does the base word mean? If you're not sure, check a dictionary.
3. Use what you know about the base word and the suffix to figure out the meaning of the unknown word.
4. Use a dictionary to check your guess.

Envision It! | **Words to Know**

landscape

miniature

prehistoric

background
reassembled

Vocabulary Strategy for

🎯 Affixes: Prefixes
pre-, re-

Word Structure A prefix is a word part that is added to the beginning of a base word. For example, *pre-* means "before." If you *prearrange* something, you arrange it before it happens. The prefix *re-* means "again." If you *reheat* soup, you warm it up again. Both *pre-* and *re-* are from Latin.

1. Look at an unfamiliar word to see if it has a base word you know.

2. Check to see if a prefix has been added to the base word.

3. Ask yourself how the prefix changes the meaning of the base word.

4. Try the meaning in the sentence. Does it make sense?

Read "Visiting the Past" on page 143. Use your knowledge of prefixes to help you determine the meanings of *prehistoric, reassembled, reproduce,* and other unfamiliar words.

Words to Write Reread "Visiting the Past." What place have you visited that uses special effects? Write a paragraph about it, using the *Words to Know.*

VISITING THE PAST

While we were on vacation, our family visited an incredible theme park. My parents had preplanned our trip to this exciting park. It had models that reproduce scenes from the past. Once we entered the park, we split up and went our own ways.

I went straight to the exhibit of prehistoric times. Paintings of huge, strange plants recreated the feeling of an ancient landscape. The model dinosaurs were life-sized, looked real, and even moved! A tape of background noises, such as animal cries and splashes, added to the realism. In one large room, artists had shaped a past world in miniature.

When we reassembled as a family for lunch, my brother described the Old West community he had visited. It had a whole street from a mining town—complete with general store, hotel, and jail. He rode a cart into a deep tunnel. Down there, the exhibit showed how miners worked. Occasionally, he said, you felt a tremor and heard a boom. Somehow they reproduced the explosions when ore was blasted from a mountain! We agreed that this was the best theme park we have ever visited.

Your Turn!

 Need a Review?
For additional help with prefixes, see page 140.

 Ready to Try It?
As you read other text, use what you learned about prefixes to help you understand it.

Envision It! | Words to Know

bluish

skidded

somersault

cartwheels   limelight

gymnastics   throbbing

hesitation   wincing

Vocabulary Strategy for

🎯 Suffixes *-ion, -ish*

Word Structure A suffix is a syllable added to the end of a root word that changes the root word's meaning. The suffix may also cause a spelling change.

For example, when *-ion*, which means "the act or state of being," is added to *appreciate*, the final *e* is dropped: *appreciation*. Another example is the Old English suffix *-ish*, which adds the meaning "somewhat" or "like," as in *brownish*.

1. Look at the unknown word. See if you recognize a root word in it.

2. Check if *-ion* or *-ish* has been added.

3. Ask yourself how the suffix changes the meaning of the root word.

4. Try the meaning in the sentence.

Read "It's Easier in Daydreams" on page 145. Look for words that end with suffixes. Analyze words and suffixes to determine word meanings.

Words to Write Reread "It's Easier in Daydreams." Imagine that you are a sports writer. Write a paragraph about a sporting event you just watched. Use words from the *Words to Know* list in your paragraph.

It's Easier in Daydreams

I love to watch Olympic gymnasts. In fact, I hope to be one myself one day. In my daydreams, I am already a star. The audience roars as I step into the limelight. Without any hesitation, I somersault across the gym. I move with terrific grace and speed. The judges smile and nod and hold up cards with perfect 10.0s on them.

So you can understand why I was so upset after what happened. I signed up for a gymnastics class offered by the park district. The teacher showed us how to do cartwheels. *This is easy!* I thought, so I didn't pay attention. When it was my turn, I ran to the mat, closed my eyes, and threw myself at it. The next thing I knew, I was flat on my back. My head and knees were throbbing. I couldn't help wincing in pain as I got up. On the next try, I lost my nerve and put on the brakes. I skidded several feet into a wall and thumped my shoulder. There's a nice bluish bruise there to remind me that I have a long way to go to reach the Olympics.

Your Turn!

 Need a Review?
For additional help with suffixes, see page 141.

 Ready to Try It?
As you read other text, use what you've learned about suffixes to help you understand it.

Envision It! | Words to Know

economic

independence

vacant

overrun

scrawled

Vocabulary Strategy for

🎯 Prefixes *over-*, *in-*

Word Structure Recognizing a prefix's meaning can help you determine the word's meaning. One of the meanings for the Old English prefix *over-* is "too much." A room that's *overcrowded* is "too crowded." The Latin prefix *in-* can mean "not." People who are *insensitive* are "not sensitive."

1. Look for a root word you know.

2. Check to see if a prefix has been added.

3. Ask yourself how the prefix changes the meaning of the root word.

4. Try the meaning in the sentence. Does it make sense?

Read "The Sky's the Limit" on page 147. Look for words with *in-* and *over-*. Use the prefixes to determine the meanings of the words.

Words to Write Reread "The Sky's the Limit." Imagine you are a reporter in the 1800s. Write an article describing why people are moving West, and how that is leading to the creation of boom towns. Use words from the *Words to Know* list.

The Sky's the Limit

Independence has always been an important value to people who live in the United States. It has been a cornerstone of American life ever since the Founding Fathers scrawled their signatures at the bottom of the Declaration of Independence.

Independence refers to people's freedoms, of course. But it also refers to their headlong way of pursuing prosperity. From all over the world, people have flocked to America in search of freedom. But many also have hoped to become rich. The building of America has been based on economic success and muscle as much as it has been based on armies and government.

This will to "make a better life" was behind the wagon trains that ventured into the West during the nineteenth century. It drove the settling of boom towns—towns that were overrun by miners. These towns grew quickly, died quickly, and soon became nothing but vacant buildings and empty streets. Every miner believed that he or she could strike it rich. The spread of railroads, then highways, recalled this theme. Every freight train chugged a message: "The sky's the limit!"

Your Turn!

❚❚ Need a Review?
For additional help with prefixes, see page 140.

▶ Ready to Try It?
As you read other text, use what you've learned about prefixes to help you understand it.

Envision It! | Words to Know

adorn

cleanse

spoonful

lifeless

precious

realm

READING STREET ONLINE
VOCABULARY ACTIVITIES
www.ReadingStreet.com

Vocabulary Strategy for

Suffixes *-less, -ful*

Word Structure A suffix is an affix added to the end of a base word that changes the base word's meaning. Sometimes the spelling of the base word changes when a suffix is added. Knowing the meaning of the suffix can help you determine the meaning of the word.

1. Look at an unfamiliar word to see if it has a base word you know.

2. Check for the suffix *-less* or *-ful*.

3. Decide how it changes the base word's meaning. The suffix *-less* can mean "without," as in *harmless*. The suffix *-ful* can mean "the amount that will fill," as in *handful*.

4. Try this meaning in the sentence to see if it makes sense.

As you read "Hospital for Wild Animals" on page 149, look for words with the suffix *-less* or *-ful*. Use the suffixes to determine the meanings of the words.

Words to Write Reread "Hospital for Wild Animals." Imagine you are the narrator. Write a short note to a friend explaining the most meaningful part of your experience. Use words from the *Words to Know* list in your note.

Hospital for
WILD ANIMALS

There are places around us where magic happens. I learned about one such place when I found an injured owl in my backyard. It had been shot in one wing. My heart sank as I bent over the apparently lifeless form. Then it moved! What could I do to save the owl?

My mom told me to call the local wildlife rehabilitation center. They told us how to carefully wrap and carry the owl to them. The worker on duty was careful to cleanse the wound. She said the owl was weak, but it might live. Over the next few weeks, I visited this magic realm every day and saw kind people helping foxes, raccoons, and birds of all kinds. Soon the helpless owl was ravenous and ate its first spoonful of meat. I saw the complex patterns of color that adorn most owls' feathers.

There was a special kind of enchantment about the place. I felt lucky to see these wild creatures up close and to be able to help them get well. It is good to know there are people who realize that the lives of wild things are precious.

Your Turn!

 Need a Review?
For additional help with suffixes, see page 141.

 Ready to Try It?
As you read other text, use what you've learned about suffixes to help you understand it.

Dictionary

A dictionary is a reference book that lists words alphabetically. It can be used to look up definitions, parts of speech, spelling, and other forms of words.

punc•tu•al ❶ (pungk' chü əl), **❷** *ADJECTIVE.*
❸ prompt; exactly on time: **❹** *He is always punctual.*
❺ ✱ *ADVERB* **punc'tu•al•ly.**

❶ Pronunciation

❷ Part of speech

❸ Definitions

❹ Example sentence

❺ Other form of the word and its part of speech

Strategy for Dictionary

1. Identify the unknown word.
2. Look up the word in a dictionary. Entries are listed alphabetically.
3. Find the part of the entry that has the information you are looking for.
4. Use the diagram above as a guide to help you locate the information you want.

Thesaurus

A thesaurus is a book of synonyms. A thesaurus will also list antonyms for many words.

cute

adjective

attractive, appealing, amusing, charming, adorable, enchanting.

ANTONYMS: plain, ugly

Strategy for Thesaurus

1. Look up the word in a thesaurus. Entries are listed alphabetically.
2. Locate the synonyms and any antonyms for your word.
3. Find the word with the exact meaning you want.

Objectives
● Use a dictionary, a glossary, or a thesaurus to locate information about words.

Envision It! | Words to Know

lair

ravine

shellfish

gnawed

headland

kelp

sinew

Vocabulary Strategy for

🎯 Unknown Words

Dictionary/Glossary Sometimes when you read, you come across a word you do not know. You can use a glossary or dictionary to find out the meaning of the word. A glossary is a list of important words and their meanings in the back of a book. A dictionary lists all words, in alphabetical order, and gives their meanings, pronunciations, syllabications, and other helpful information.

1. Find the word in a dictionary.

2. Read the pronunciation to yourself.

3. Read all the meanings given for the word.

4. Choose the meaning that makes sense in your sentence.

Read "Island Survival" on page 153. Use a dictionary to help you determine the meanings, pronunciations, and syllabications of the *Words to Know*.

Words to Write Reread "Island Survival." Write a story about a wild animal that lives on an island. Use words from the *Words to Know* list in your story.

Island Survival

Have you ever imagined being shipwrecked on an island? What would you do to survive? First, you would take a look around to see how you could get food, water, and shelter. A lot would depend on what kind of land your island had.

A rocky, hilly island might have a cave you could use as your home—unless it was already a lair for a wild animal. As you explored, you would keep an eye out for things you could use for building or for hunting. Small trees growing in a ravine might be cut down to build a lean-to.

If you were able to hunt game, you might save parts of animals to use in your home. After you gnawed the flesh, you would have hides to make a blanket. Sinew could serve as a kind of rope. In shallow waters you would find shellfish to eat. The kelp floating there could be used as "wallpaper" or even as food.

If your island had a headland, it would provide a good high point from which to look out for rescue. You might build a fire there to draw the attention of passing ships.

Your Turn!

 Need a Review?
For additional help with using a dictionary, see page 150.

 Ready to Try It?
As you read other text, use a dictionary or glossary to find the meanings of unknown words.

Envision It! | **Words to Know**

canteen

glory

stallion

confederacy

quarrel

rebellion

union

Vocabulary Strategy for

🎯 Unknown Words

Dictionary/Glossary When you read, you may come across a word you do not know. You can use a glossary or dictionary to find out the meaning of the word. A glossary lists and defines important words in a book. A dictionary lists all words, in alphabetical order, and gives their meanings, pronunciations, and other information.

1. Use a print or electronic dictionary to find the entry for a word.

2. Read the pronunciation to yourself. Saying the word may help you recognize it.

3. Read all the meanings given for the word.

4. Choose the meaning that makes sense in your sentence.

As you read "Civil War Drummers," use a dictionary to look up the meanings of the *Words to Know*.

Words to Write Reread "Civil War Drummers." Imagine you are a war drummer. Write a paragraph describing your experience. Use words from the *Words to Know* list.

Civil War DRUMMERS

In the Civil War, both the Union army and the army of the Confederacy relied on their drummers. The drummers were an essential part of their battles.

The Civil War was much more than a quarrel between the North and the South. It was a war, with fierce battles fought on the ground. For this reason, drummers were needed, and not just to play marching beats. Drummers were needed on the battlefield to alert soldiers when to retreat to safety. An officer mounted on his stallion would lean down to tell his drummer to play a drum call for a charge or some other troop movement. Off the battlefield, the **drummers'** beats alerted officers to planning **meetings**.

War drummers had to be brave. They marched onto the battlefield unarmed, carrying just their water canteens and their drums. Perhaps the drummers didn't get the glory that the soldiers did, but they performed important work for both the North and the South, as they fought during the rebellion.

Your Turn!

 Need a Review?
For additional help with using a dictionary, see page 150.

 Ready to Try It?
As you read other text, use a dictionary or glossary to find the meanings of unknown words.

Envision It! | Words to Know

debris

robotic

sonar

cramped

interior

ooze

sediment

Vocabulary Strategy for

🎯 Unknown Words

Dictionary/Glossary Sometimes a writer doesn't include context clues in the sentences surrounding an unknown word. In this case, you have to look up the word in a dictionary or glossary. Follow these steps.

1. Look to see whether the book has a glossary. If not, use a dictionary. You can use a printed or electronic dictionary.

2. Find the word entry. If the pronunciation is given, read it aloud. You may recognize the word when you hear yourself say it.

3. Look at all the meanings listed in the entry. Try each meaning in the sentence that contains the unknown word.

4. Choose the meaning that makes sense in your sentence.

Read "In the Ocean Deeps" on page 157. Use a dictionary to determine the meanings of words you cannot figure out from the text.

Words to Write Reread "In the Ocean Deeps." Write a paragraph about a similar scientific experiment. Use words from the *Words to Know* list in your paragraph.

IN THE OCEAN DEEPS

What lies in the ocean deeps and what lives there? Scientists work hard to answer those questions. The ocean floor is miles deep in many places. It is very cold and dark down there. The pressure of so much water would crush divers instantly. How can they get down there to find answers?

Scientists use high-tech machines. A sonar system sends out beeps of sound that bounce off the ocean floor. Computers can use the beeps to make maps. Scientists look at the maps for areas that interest them. Then they send down submersible vehicles that can withstand the high pressure. Many of these vehicles are robotic. They carry cameras and other equipment to record what it is like down there. At great depths, they may show an ooze of melted rock coming from deep inside the Earth. They may show a "desert" of sediment or a mountain range.

Some of these deep-sea machines carry divers. The interior of one of these machines is small, so scientists are cramped. But that is a small price to pay to be able to see **for themselves** the wonders of deep-sea life. Strange **and** wonderful plants and animals have **been** discovered far below the surface. Sadly, so have debris, trash, and damage done by pollution.

Your Turn!

 Need a Review?
For additional help with using a dictionary, see page 150.

 Ready to Try It?
As you read other text, use a dictionary or glossary to find the meanings of unknown words.

Objectives

• Use a dictionary, a glossary, or a thesaurus to locate information about words.

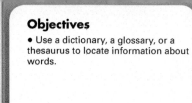

Words to Know

bizarre

headline

Monday July 21 1969

9: Man makes his first sp

On the moon
fter perfect
ouchdown

roost

breathtaking

high-pitched

vital

Vocabulary Strategy for

🎯 Unknown Words

Dictionary/Glossary Sometimes a writer doesn't include context clues in the sentences surrounding an unknown word. In this case, you have to look up the word in a dictionary or glossary to find its meaning, pronunciation, part of speech, and syllabication. When you come across an unknown word, follow these steps.

1. Check the back of the book for a glossary, or use a dictionary.

2. Find the word entry. If the pronunciation and syllabication are given, read the word aloud. You may recognize the word when you hear yourself say it.

3. Look at all the meanings and parts of speech listed in the entry. Try each meaning in the sentence that contains the unknown word.

4. Choose the meaning that makes sense in your sentence.

Read "Ears for Eyes" on page 159. Use a dictionary to determine the meanings of words you cannot figure out from the text.

Words to Write Reread "Ears for Eyes." Think of other mammals that hunt at night and write an article about them. Use words from the *Words to Know* list in your article.

Ears for Eyes

What do bats and dolphins have in common? It's certainly not where they live! It's echolocation, the process of using sound to "see" in the dark. Instead of relying on eyesight, these mammals locate prey with high-pitched sounds, creating for each other a breathtaking symphony.

Echolocation is bizarre, and you won't read explanations of it in newspaper headlines. Here's how it works. Mammals that use echolocation listen to the differences in sound between their right and left ears to locate objects. As sounds emitted by the mammals bounce off an object and come back, the mammals keep track of the time it takes for the sound to reflect off the object. In this way, they are able to calculate where their prey is—all in a matter of seconds!

It might seem strange that mammals use their ears instead of their eyes to locate prey. Why do they? For one, echolocation provides them an ecological advantage. For example, if bats can roost during the day and hunt at night, they can take advantage of prey when it is vulnerable. Also, bats can hunt while their predators are sleeping. Indeed, echolocation is vital to these mammals' survival.

Your Turn!

 Need a Review?
For additional help with using a dictionary, see page 150.

 Ready to Try It?
As you read other text, use a dictionary or glossary to find the meanings of unknown words.

Multiple-Meaning Words

Multiple-meaning words are words that have different meanings depending on how they are used. Homonyms, homographs, and homophones are all multiple-meaning words.

Homographs

Homographs are words that are spelled the same but have different meanings and are sometimes pronounced differently.

Wind

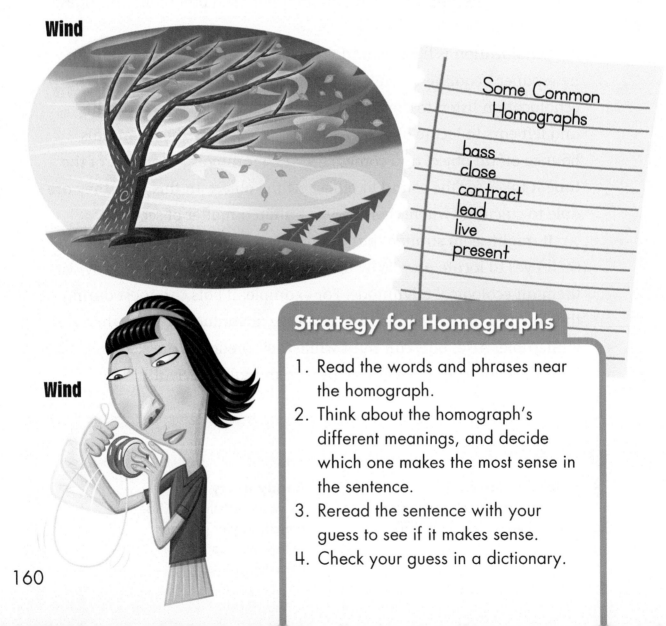

Some Common Homographs

bass
close
contract
lead
live
present

Wind

Strategy for Homographs

1. Read the words and phrases near the homograph.
2. Think about the homograph's different meanings, and decide which one makes the most sense in the sentence.
3. Reread the sentence with your guess to see if it makes sense.
4. Check your guess in a dictionary.

Homonyms

Homonyms are words that are pronounced the same and have the same spelling, but their meanings are different.

Pitcher

Pitcher

Some Common Homonyms

pen
duck
mail
ear
bank
bark

Strategy for Homonyms

1. Read the words and phrases near the homonym.
2. Think about the homonym's different meanings, and decide which one makes the most sense.
3. Reread the sentence with your guess to see if it makes sense.
4. Use a dictionary to check your guess.

Homophones

Homophones are words that are pronounced the same way but have different spellings and meanings.

Eight

Ate

Some Common
Homophones

ate	eight
bored	board
brake	break
knight	night
weight	wait

Strategy for Homophones

1. Think about the different spellings and meanings of the homophone.
2. Check a dictionary for the definitions of the words.
3. Use the word that best fits your writing.

This chart can help you remember the differences between homographs, homonyms, and homophones.

Understanding Homographs, Homonyms, and Homophones

	Pronunciation	Spelling	Meaning
Homographs	may be the same or different	same	different
Homonyms	same	same	different
Homophones	same	different	different

address

Homograph

address

duck

Homonym

duck

Homophone bear

bare

Envision It! | Words to Know

compressions

minute

neutral

grumbled

insistently

intentionally

normally

Vocabulary Strategy for

🎯 Homographs

Context Clues Homographs are words that are spelled the same but have different meanings and sometimes have different pronunciations. For example, *bass* (rhymes with *face*) is a musical instrument, while *bass* (rhymes with *class*) is a type of fish. Use context clues to determine which word (and meaning) is being used. Follow these steps.

1. Read the words and sentences around the homograph.

2. Think about its possible meaning.

3. Reread the sentence and put in one of the meanings.

4. See if the meaning makes sense in the sentence. If not, try another meaning.

Read "Lifesaving Classes" on page 165. Look for homographs. Use context clues to help you figure out the meanings. Use a dictionary to determine how the words are pronounced.

Words to Write Reread "Lifesaving Classes." Write a paragraph about the job of a lifeguard. Describe how lifeguards prepare and what they need to know. Use words from the *Words to Know* list in your writing.

LIFESAVING Classes

Normally I spend my summers at my best friend's cottage, but this summer is different. I want to get a job as a lifeguard, so I have to take classes and practice swimming. When I heard that first aid was going to be one of the classes, I grumbled out loud. I don't like the sight of blood. I intentionally avoided looking at the screen during a film about how to wrap wounds. My teacher noticed and insistently asked me about the proper techniques to stop excessive bleeding.

I liked the class about CPR (cardiopulmonary resuscitation), because CPR can really save a person's life. I was surprised by how tiring it is. It is best to work with a partner so that you can take turns doing compressions and rescue breaths. In a drowning case, every minute matters.

Some of the other classes that I'll take this summer are boat safety, rescue diving, and crowd control. I already know how to put the boat in forward, neutral, and reverse from spending summers at my friend's cottage on a lake. I am going to miss hanging out with her, but I'm very excited about becoming a lifeguard.

Your Turn!

 Need a Review?
For additional help with homographs, see page 160.

 Ready to Try It?
As you read other text, use what you've learned about homographs to help you understand it.

Envision It! Words to Know

branded

constructed

devastation

daintily   resourceful
lullaby   thieving
pitch   veins

Vocabulary Strategy for

🎯 Homonyms

Context Clues When you read, you may come across homonyms. Homonyms are words that are spelled the same but have different meanings. For example, *feet* can mean "units of measurement" or "the end parts of the legs." You can use context clues to determine or clarify which meaning is being used.

1. Reread the sentence in which the homonym appears.

2. Look for clues to the homonym's meaning.

3. If you need more help, read the sentences around the sentence with the homonym.

4. Try the meaning in the sentence. Does it make sense?

Read "The Tale of Carrie the Calf" on page 167. Use context clues to help you determine or clarify the meanings of homonyms you find.

Words to Write Reread "The Tale of Carrie the Calf." Imagine you are Carrie the Calf. Write a story in the first person about a typical day in your unusual life. Use words from the *Words to Know* list in your story.

The Tale of Carrie the Calf

From the moment she was born, we knew Carrie the Calf was different. Her eyes were as black as pitch, and she was as strong as a bull. Instead of blood, she seemed to have a magic potion in her veins. Overnight, she grew fifty feet tall. Morning found her daintily eating the tops of trees.

It was hard getting enough for her to eat! We would give her one hundred bales of hay for breakfast, but by lunch she would be over at the next ranch, eating its trees and anything else in sight. This thieving did not make her too popular. It also caused considerable devastation around the country. Then the time came to brand the calves! How could a 150-foot-tall calf be branded? We quickly constructed a 200-foot-tall fence to hold her in. She just smiled, hopped over it, and then ambled off to find another forest to eat. To catch Carrie, we needed to be more resourceful.

Next, we made a set of speakers as big as a house. We broadcasted a soothing lullaby that could be heard over three states. Soon Carrie was sleeping without a care.

Your Turn!

 Need a Review?
For additional help with homonyms, see page 161.

 Ready to Try It?
As you read other text, use what you've learned about homonyms to help you understand it.

Envision It! | Words to Know

barren

deafening

prying

lurched

previous

surveying

Vocabulary Strategy for

Multiple-Meaning Words

Context Clues Some words have more than one meaning. You can find clues in nearby words and sentences to decide which meaning the author is using. These context clues can help you determine or clarify the meaning of a multiple-meaning word.

1. Think about different meanings the word can have.

2. Reread the sentence in which the word appears. Which meaning fits?

3. If you can't tell, then look for more clues in nearby sentences.

4. Put the clues together and decide which meaning works best.

Read "A New Place to Live" on page 169. Use the context to decide which meaning a multiple-meaning word has in the article.

Words to Write Reread "A New Place to Live." Imagine you are a construction worker building a skyscraper. Write a journal entry describing what you see and hear as you work. Use words from the *Words to Know* list in your journal entry.

A New Place to Live

On Tuesday, the foreman started his day by surveying the barren lot between two existing homes. His crew of workers had done a great job the previous day clearing away the old home. He felt confident that this crew could accomplish his goal. He wanted to build a brand-new house within a month.

The workers were ready for the challenge. The foreman explained what he wanted finished by the end of each day. Today he wanted the ground prepared for a foundation. Every crew member knew his or her job. The first sound was the prying open of the bulldozer door. This was followed by the deafening sound of the jackhammers as they broke up an old sidewalk. The bulldozer lurched forward and began to pile dirt in one spot. Teams of workers carried lumber from a truck to the lot. Everywhere the foreman looked, he smiled.

Your Turn!

 Need a Review?
For additional help with multiple-meaning words, see pages 160–163.

 Ready to Try It?
As you read other text, use what you've learned about multiple-meaning words to help you understand it.

Envision It! | Words to Know

applauds

inspecting

project

browsing

fabulous

Vocabulary Strategy for

🔄 Multiple-Meaning Words

Context Clues Some words have more than one meaning. Use words and sentences around the word with multiple meanings to figure out which meaning the author is using.

1. When you find a multiple-meaning word, read the context clues around it.

2. Think about the different meanings the word has. For example, the word *crop* can mean "a product grown for food" or "to cut short."

3. Reread the sentence, replacing the word with one of the meanings.

4. If this meaning does not work, try another meaning of the word.

Read "The Play's the Thing" on page 171. Use context clues to help you determine and clarify the meanings of multiple-meaning words.

Words to Write Reread "The Play's the Thing." Write a note to a friend explaining why you would like to see a play. Use words from the *Words to Know* list in your note.

The Play's the Thing

Writing a play is hard work. But it can also be an enjoyable project for an author—and the audience. An author creates a whole new world, and then fills it with people who do what he or she wishes. The author can use them to tell realistic stories, or send them off on fabulous adventures.

The next time you are browsing in the library, look for famous plays. Notice the way that authors describe their characters. How do they look and sound? Look at the stage directions. They tell you how the characters will move and what will be around them.

If you get a chance, go to a play. It can be lots of fun. Inspecting the stage before the play starts will tell you something about the mood the author wants to create. When the actors come on stage, this fantasy world comes alive.

As the play ends and the audience applauds, the author often feels a real sense of joy. So does the crowd. They were able to escape—even for a little while—to a different world.

Your Turn!

 Need a Review?
For additional help with multiple-meaning words, see pages 160–163.

 Ready to Try It?
As you read other text, use what you've learned about multiple-meaning words to help you understand it.

Envision It! | **Words to Know**

mold

tidied

workshop

erected

foundations

occasion

proportion

READING STREET ONLINE
VOCABULARY ACTIVITIES
www.ReadingStreet.com

Vocabulary Strategy for

🎯 Homonyms

Context Clues Homonyms are words with the same spelling but different origins and meanings. You can use context to help figure out their meanings. The words and sentences around the homonym offer clues.

1. Read the words and sentences around the homonym to find clues.

2. Think about the homonym's different meanings. For example, the word *bill* can mean "a statement of money owed" or "the beak of a bird."

3. Try each meaning in the sentence and decide which meaning makes sense.

Read "The Artist of the Hour" on page 173. Use context clues to help you determine and clarify the meanings of homonyms.

Words to Write Reread "The Artist of the Hour." How would you make a model of a dinosaur? Write an explanation and the steps in your plan. Use words from the *Words to Know* list in your writing.

The Artist of the Hour

Imagine that you are an artist at work in your workshop. You have been asked to make a sculpture for the new hospital. When people look at this sculpture, they are supposed to think about freedom and hope. You have decided to make a group of birds in flight.

First, you make a clay shape of each bird. You must measure carefully to be sure the proportion of the wings to the body is just right. Then you cover the shapes with melted plastic and let it get hard. Each mold has the exact shape of the bird you made. Next, you pour cement into each mold. After it hardens, any crumbs of cement and plastic must be tidied up. Then you have a whole bird shape.

Meanwhile, you have to build foundations for the birds. These are bases made of wood or cement, with iron pipes sticking up. When they are fastened to the rods, the birds will look as though they are sailing into the sky.

You hope your work of art will be erected in the flower garden at the hospital. When it is put in place, you will be honored for your work. There will be a party to celebrate the occasion.

Your Turn!

 Need a Review?
For additional help with homonyms, see page 161.

 Ready to Try It?
As you read other text, use what you've learned about homonyms to help you understand it.

Envision It! | Words to Know

accomplishments

gravity

monitors

focus

role

specific

Vocabulary Strategy for

Multiple-Meaning Words

Context Clues Some words have more than one meaning. You can find context clues in nearby words to determine and clarify which meaning the author is using. Follow these steps.

1. Think about the different meanings the word can have.

2. Reread the sentence in which the word appears. Did you find any context clues? Which meaning fits in the sentence?

3. If you can't tell, look for more clues in nearby sentences.

4. Put the clues together and decide which meaning works best.

Read "To Be an Astronaut" on page 175. Use the context to decide which meaning a multiple-meaning word has in the article. For example, does the word *role* mean "a character in a play" or "a pattern of behavior"?

Words to Write Reread "To Be an Astronaut." Write a paragraph about what you think space travel will be like in the future. Be sure to use the correct meanings of each of the words from the *Words to Know* list in your paragraph.

To Be an Astronaut

Astronauts have a special place in our history. They are people of special character too. Like all explorers, astronauts must be curious and brave. As scientists, they must be well trained in physics and math with a focus on astronomy. They are also skilled pilots.

To live in space, astronauts must be in top shape. Because there is no gravity in space, they must get used to being weightless. Each flight brings different jobs with specific assignments. One time, astronauts may build part of a space station. Another time, they may carry out dozens of tests. They may have to use a robot arm and watch what the arm is doing on monitors. The computer screens let them adjust the arm's movements. These are only a few of the many tasks astronauts must accomplish in space.

Astronauts have many accomplishments, but none are more important than serving as positive role models for young people. These space explorers' courage, learning, and devotion to duty make them shining examples. They show us that people may reach for the stars.

Your Turn!

Need a Review?
For additional help with multiple-meaning words, see pages 160–163.

Ready to Try It?
As you read other text, use what you've learned about multiple-meaning words to help you understand it.

175

Envision It! | Words to Know

clarinet

jammed

nighttime

bass

fidgety

forgetful

secondhand

Vocabulary Strategy for

🎯 Homographs

Context Clues Homographs are words that are spelled the same but have different meanings. Some homographs also have different pronunciations. For example, *minute* (MIN-it) means "sixty seconds," while *minute* (my-NOOT) means "tiny." Use the words and sentences around a homograph to determine and clarify which word (and meaning) is being used.

1. Read the words and sentences around the homograph.

2. Think about its possible meanings.

3. Reread the sentence and put in one of the meanings.

4. See if the meaning makes sense in the sentence. If not, try another meaning for the homograph.

Read "Jazz in Harlem" on page 177. Use the words and sentences around a homograph to determine and clarify which meaning the author is using.

Words to Write Reread "Jazz in Harlem." Imagine you can hear jazz music as you read. Write a description of the music. Use words from the *Words to Know* list in your description.

Jazz in Harlem

No history of black Harlem would be complete without talking about culture. In writing, art, and music, African American creators shone. In no area was that light brighter than in jazz. It grew out of the blues and ragtime. It was wild and free and toe-tapping. In the 1920s in Harlem, the nighttime was alive with this music.

Great musicians such as Louis Armstrong and Duke Ellington jammed far into the night. The sounds of trumpet, drums, clarinet, and bass spilled from the nightclubs. The jazz they played had big muscles and a big heart. It wanted to dance. Never mind that some of the instruments were secondhand, and the musicians didn't make as much money as they deserved.

Crowds listened with rapt attention. From the most forgetful old-timer to the most fidgety baby, people soaked up the music as if it were sunshine. Harlem in the 1920s was a place for African Americans to show their culture and their spirit.

Your Turn!

Need a Review?

For additional help with homographs, see page 160.

Ready to Try It?

As you read other text, use what you've learned about homographs to help you understand it.

177

Base Words/Root Words

A base word, also called a root word, is a word that can't be broken into smaller words.

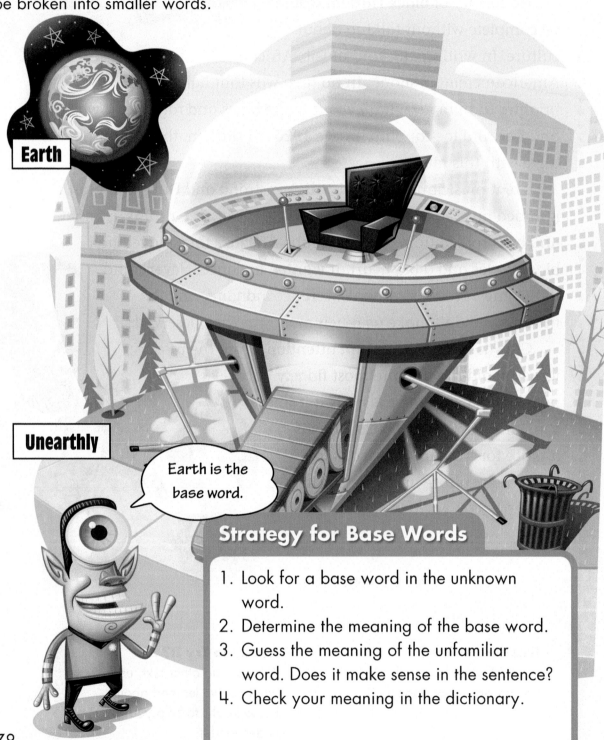

Earth

Unearthly

Earth is the base word.

Strategy for Base Words

1. Look for a base word in the unknown word.
2. Determine the meaning of the base word.
3. Guess the meaning of the unfamiliar word. Does it make sense in the sentence?
4. Check your meaning in the dictionary.

178

Word Origins: Roots

Many English words contain Greek and Latin roots.

Telescope

Automobile

Television

Latin Roots

dent	tooth
dict	to say; to speak
scrib	to write
sub	under; below
tract	to pull
vis	to see

Greek Roots

auto	self
bio	life
micro	very small
ology	the study of
phon	sound; voice
scope	see
tele	far

Strategy for Roots

1. Using what you know about roots, guess the meaning of the unknown word.
2. Does your guess make sense in the sentence?
3. Use a dictionary to check your guess.

astonished

gratitude

procession

behavior

benefactor

distribution

recommend

sacred

traditions

Vocabulary Strategy for

Greek and Latin Roots

Word Structure When you come to an unknown word, particularly an academic vocabulary word, look for a root within the word. For example, the Latin root *bene* means "well" or "good," as in *benefit* and *benefactor*. The Greek root *myth* means "fable" or "legend," as in *myth* and *mythology*. You can use roots to figure out the meaning of an unknown word.

1. Find a root in the word. Think about other words you know that also have this root.

2. Do the words you know give you clues about the meaning of the unknown word?

3. Check to see if the meaning makes sense in the sentence.

Read "The Meaning of Tales" on page 181. Look for roots to help you figure out the meanings of the *Words to Know* or words such as *mysterious, triumph,* or *celebrate.*

Words to Write Reread "The Meaning of Tales." Write a myth or tale of your own that explains something or teaches a lesson about life. Use words from the *Words to Know* list.

The Meaning of Tales

Myths, fairy tales, and folk tales are time-honored traditions in many countries. Before people could write, they told stories to make each other laugh, cry, or shake with fear. These stories do more than just entertain. They preserve the earliest ideas and history of a people. A myth may explain why something happens in nature. It may tell what causes the seasons, for example. A tale may show us the rewards for our behavior and teach us a lesson. Often, both myths and tales are tied to what people in earlier times found sacred and mysterious.

Fairy tales reach into the world of fancy. A poor girl finds a benefactor, such as a fairy godmother. A handsome prince discovers the girl and is astonished by her beauty. They fall in love. Someone evil tears them apart, and they suffer great misery. A magic being helps them defeat the evil. They feel a joyful gratitude. They celebrate their triumph in a grand procession through the kingdom. The distribution of these stories all over the world shows how important they are to all people. Do you want to understand the nature of people? I recommend that you study tales.

Your Turn!

❚❚ Need a Review?

For additional help with Greek and Latin roots, see page 179.

▶ Ready to Try It?

As you read other text, use what you've learned about Greek and Latin roots to help you understand it.

fearless

glimmer

somber

fate

lingers

magnified

steed

Vocabulary Strategy for

🔄 Endings *-s, -ed, -ing*

Word Structure The endings *-s, -ed,* and *-ing* come from Old English and may be added to a verb to change the tense, person, or usage of the verb. You can use these endings to help you figure out the meanings of *lingers* and *magnified*.

1. Cover the ending and read the base form of the word.

2. Reread the sentence and make sure the word is a verb. (Nouns can also end in *-s*.)

3. Now look in the sentence for clues about what the word may mean.

4. See if your meaning makes sense in the sentence.

Read "War Heroes in Stone" on page 183. Look for verbs that end with *-s, -ed,* or *-ing*. Think about the endings and the way the words are used to help you figure out the words' meanings.

Words to Write Reread "War Heroes in Stone." Write a paragraph describing a statue you've seen. Describe what it looks like and what it represents. Use words from the *Words to Know* list in your writing.

War Heroes in Stone

Monuments to war heroes have a noble feeling. Artists who make statues to honor the war dead seem to understand their job. Soldiers who died in battle gave their lives for their country and for freedom. The somber job of the artist is to honor these heroes. Artists also want us to feel proud of what these heroes did. The artists' work is one way of giving thanks to those who met their fate on the field of battle.

Often the statue shows a general sitting on his steed, sword raised overhead. The marble forms are beautiful, powerful, and larger than life. In addition, the statue sits high on a pedestal so that visitors must look up. Both horse and man are a study in fearless forward motion. In this way, their bravery and patriotism are magnified and set in stone.

Have you ever seen such a statue at night? Imagine the white stone looming in the dark. Then a glimmer of moonlight brings it to life. The effect is strange to see. You feel you can almost hear the tread of troops marching down a dusty road. The distant sound of marching lingers in the air. You send a silent word of thanks to those who fought to keep your country free.

Your Turn!

 Need a Review?
For additional help with base words and endings, see page 178.

 Ready to Try It?
As you read other text, use what you've learned about word endings to help you understand it.

Envision It! | Words to Know

architect

bronze

cannon

achieved

depressed

fashioned

midst

philosopher

rival

Vocabulary Strategy for

🎯 Greek and Latin Roots

Word Structure Many words in English are based on Greek and Latin roots. For example, the Greek root *bio* means "life." The Latin word *canna* means "reed or tube." When you see a longer word you do not understand, look for a root that can help you figure out the meaning.

1. Look at the word. Try to identify its root.

2. Think of words you know where this same root appears, and then try to determine a meaning for the word.

3. Try the meaning in place of the unfamiliar word, and see if it makes sense in the sentence.

Read "They Called It the Renaissance." Use your knowledge of Greek and Latin roots to help you determine the meanings of words such as *architect*, *philosopher*, or *achieved*.

Words to Write Reread "They Called It the Renaissance." Write a paragraph about why you think architecture was important to people during the Renaissance. Use words from the *Words to Know* list in your writing.

They Called It the RENAISSANCE

The Middle Ages ran from about 500 A.D. to about 1450 A.D. This was a time that might have depressed anyone. People in Europe looked back at the past instead of forward to the future.

But by 1450, people had stopped thinking only about the past and started looking ahead to what might be achieved in the future. This new age was known as the Renaissance.

Inventors started coming up with exciting new inventions. The title *philosopher* became important again, as thinkers explored new ways to enrich people's lives. The architect became an important figure as beautiful new buildings took shape in cities and towns across Europe. Artists fashioned powerful sculptures and painted vivid paintings that looked natural and real.

In the midst of all this growth and change, of course, there was still fighting. Art was the glory of the age, but war was the harsh reality. Bronze might be used to make a beautiful statue or a deadly cannon. People were sailing off to find new lands. A nation might become a rival of another nation, fighting for land in the Americas. In so many ways, people in the Renaissance were preparing for the modern world.

Your Turn!

 Need a Review?
For additional help with Greek and Latin roots, see page 179.

 Ready to Try It?
As you read other text, use what you've learned about Greek and Latin roots to help you understand it.

Envision It! | **Words to Know**

civilization

complex

fleeing

blunders
envy
inspired
rustling
strategy

Vocabulary Strategy for

Endings *-ed, -ing, -s*

Word Structure The Old English endings *-ed* and *-ing* may be added to verbs to change the tense, person, or usage of the verb. The *-s* ending has the same function. You can use endings to help determine the meaning of an unknown word.

1. Examine the unknown word to see if it has a root word you know.

2. Check to see if the ending *-ed, -ing,* or *-s* has been added to a base word. Remember that some base words drop the final *-e* before adding an ending. For example, *rustle* becomes *rustling*.

3. Reread the sentence and make sure the word shows action. (The ending *-s* may be added to nouns too.)

4. Decide how the ending changes the meaning of the base word.

5. Try the meaning in the sentence.

Read "Long-Ago Lives" on page 187. Look for words that end with *-ed, -ing,* or *-s*. Use the endings to help determine the words' meanings.

Words to Write Reread "Long-Ago Lives." Imagine that you are living in an ancient civilization. Write about what you see. Use words from the *Words to Know* list in your writing.

LONG-AGO LIVES

We do not usually envy the lives of people who lived thousands of years ago. We are likely to imagine them fleeing for their lives from enemies or wild beasts. Any civilization without excellent shopping, television, and computers seems far too primitive for us.

However, we have learned much about early cultures. What we have learned shows us that their world was often complex, not simple. They were not all that different from us. For example, two thousand years ago the Mayan people played a ball game. The game was played by teams on stone courts with special goals. Players needed great strength and skill. The strategy was to send a heavy ball through a high stone ring using only hips, knees, and elbows. Kings might play this game, for which the stakes were very high. No one wanted to make any blunders because the loser might lose his head!

This game may have inspired our modern game of soccer. Stand on one of those ancient ball courts and you can almost feel the excitement of the crowd or hear the rustling of a feather headdress.

Your Turn!

 Need a Review?
For additional help with base words and endings, see page 178.

 Ready to Try It?
As you read other text, use what you've learned about word endings to help you understand it.

bellow

feat

savage

abandoned

attempt

cavern

immensely

Vocabulary Strategy for

Greek and Latin Roots

Word Structure Greek and Latin roots are words or parts of words from the Greek and Latin languages. For example, *excavation* comes from the Latin prefix *ex-,* meaning "out of," the Latin root *cave,* meaning "hollow," and the Latin suffix *-ation,* meaning "act or process of." *Excavation* means "the act or process of hollowing out."

When you come across a difficult word, follow these steps:

1. Look for a root in the word. See if you recognize the root. Do you know another word that has this root?

2. See whether the root meaning of the known word gives you a clue about the meaning of the unknown word.

3. Then check to see if this meaning makes sense in the sentence.

Read "The Cave in the Cliff" on page 189. Look for Greek and Latin roots and affixes you can use to determine the meanings of words such as *prehistoric, antitourist,* or other unknown words.

Words to Write Reread "The Cave in the Cliff." Write a paragraph about discovering a cave. Use words from the *Words to Know* list in your paragraph.

The Cave in the Cliff

Ryan reached a ledge on the cliff and looked down at the height he had scaled. "What an amazing climbing feat!" he said to his father. He was immensely proud of himself.

Then Ryan turned around to notice a large cavern opening in the side of cliff. "Look, Dad. A cave!" he said.

Dad clambered up onto the ledge. "Let's inspect it," he said, and he and Ryan entered the cave. "I see signs of excavation near the back," Dad commented. "Somebody was digging, probably in an attempt to make the cave deeper. The dig was apparently abandoned years ago, though."

"Somebody has drawn on the wall," said Ryan. He pointed to a picture of a prehistoric, savage-looking beast.

They heard a loud bellow from the bottom of the cliff. Ryan could not distinguish the individual words, but he guessed that his brother was calling them to dinner.

They got ready to climb down.

"Shall we tell people about this cave?" asked Ryan.

"No, people might come and spoil it. I don't mean to be antitourist, but let's leave it as is," said Dad.

Your Turn!

 Need a Review?
For additional help with Greek and Latin roots, see page 179.

 Ready to Try It?
As you read other text, use what you've learned about Greek and Latin roots to help you understand it.

189

Envision It! | **Words to Know**

decay

parasites

tundra

bleached

carcasses

scrawny

starvation

suspicions

Vocabulary Strategy for

🎯 Endings -s, -es

Word Structure An ending is a letter or letters added to the end of a base word that changes how the word is used. For example, the endings -s and -es from Old English make singular nouns plural. Recognizing an ending may help you determine the meaning of a word.

1. Look at the unknown word to see if it has a base word you know.

2. Check to see if the ending -s or -es has been added.

3. Ask yourself how the ending changes the meaning of the base word.

4. See if the meaning makes sense in the sentence.

Read "Cleanup by Mother Nature" on page 191. Look for words ending in -s or -es. Use the endings to determine the meanings of the words.

Words to Write Reread "Cleanup by Mother Nature." Imagine you are a scientist talking about the life cycle of animals. Write a speech that explains the ideas from the selection. Use words from the *Words to Know* list in your speech.

CLEANUP BY
MOTHER NATURE

All living things die. This is not a pleasant fact. Most people do not think about it very often. Seeing the carcasses of animals that have been hit on the road can be a startling reminder.

Some animals die to provide food for other animals. Perhaps you have seen a scrawny wild animal. This arouses suspicions in your mind that the animal is unhealthy. It may die from starvation, sickness, or parasites, such as worms, that live off its tissues. Many house pets pass through their entire life cycle and die of old age. What happens to the bodies of animals when they die?

In nature, nothing is wasted. Whether in the frozen tundra or the steamy jungles, bodies of dead animals are broken down. Through the process of decay, their tissues are changed into simpler chemicals. These chemicals go into the soil, and plants use them. Soon all that can be seen of a dead animal are bleached bones. In time, these break down and disappear as well.

Your Turn!

 Need a Review?
For additional help with base words and endings, see page 178.

 Ready to Try It?
As you read other text, use what you've learned about base words and endings to help you understand it.

Fiction
folk tale
historical fiction
legend
myth
novel
realistic fiction
tall tale

Drama

Poetry

Informational Text
expository text
persuasive text
procedural text

Literary Nonfiction
autobiography
biography

Genre

As you read,
- decide if a selection is fiction or nonfiction.
- think about character, setting, plot, and theme.
- think about how the information in a selection is presented.

Literature is classified into different types, or genres. Knowing about genres can help you better understand what you read. It can also help you choose what to read when you read independently.

Ready to Try It? ▶

Fiction describes imaginary events or people.

Genre	A **folk tale** is a story or legend that is handed down from one generation to the next. It usually has no known author.	**Historical fiction** is a made-up story that takes place in the past.	A **legend** is a well-known story that takes place in the past and contains exaggerated people or events.
Setting	A folk tale usually takes place "long ago and far away."	The setting is a real place or like a real place. It has a specific focus on a time and place in history.	The story takes place in the past, but places are usually real.
Characters	The characters are flat, or simple. They may be capable of superhuman actions. They may be portrayed as "good" or "bad."	Characters are like real people or based on real people. They fit in with the historical time and place.	Characters are heroes with superhuman actions or deeds. They are often fictional versions of people in history.
Plot	The conflict is usually between two or more characters, or between characters and nature.	The story can have any kind of conflict, but it is often about a challenge in society that characters must overcome, or about a great accomplishment.	The plot can be any conflict involving the hero character.

Genre	A **myth** is a tale handed down by word of mouth. Myths may explain life, human behavior, or events in nature. Like fables, they can teach lessons.	A **novel** is a longer fictional story, often divided into chapters. Novels can be realistic, historical, science fiction, fantasy, and so on.
Setting	The story is usually set in a fictional past. It begins "Long ago…" or "There once was…"	The time of a novel can be any time, and the place of a novel can be any place.
Characters	Animals and things in nature, such as wind, can talk, think, and act like people.	Main characters are well developed. Readers learn more about the characters as the story is told.
Plot	The plot is often a conflict between two or more characters, or between characters and nature.	Side plots or subplots are common. A novel may tell several side stories that connect to the main plot.

Fiction describes imaginary events or people.

	Realistic fiction	Tall tale
Genre	**Realistic fiction** is a made-up story that could really happen. An adventure story is one example of realistic fiction.	A **tall tale** is a humorous, exaggerated story with unbelievable events and characters.
Setting	The setting is in a real place or in a place that seems real. The story may take place in the past or present.	A tall tale often takes place in the past, sometimes in real places.
Characters	Characters think, talk, and act like real people.	Characters have superhuman abilities. Sometimes they are fictional versions of people in history.
Plot	The plot is realistic and believable.	The story can be about anything. It may also explain why or how something exists as it does today.

Drama and **poetry** tell a real or fictional story in a unique way.

Genre	**Drama** tells a story that is meant to be performed.	**Poetry** is verse arranged in lines that have rhythm and may rhyme.
Features	Characters' dialogue and stage directions tell the story. There is information on characters and the setting.	Poetry has lines of text that are rhythmic. It has descriptive words, sound effects, and other poetic elements.
Organization	Drama is organized by lines of dialogue and stage directions.	A poem can have any organization. It may be organized in groups of lines called stanzas that use line breaks, rhyme, and meter.
Includes...	plays; sketches; skits; scripts for radio or television; dramatic adaptations	limericks; cinquains; haikus; ballads; humorous rhyming poems; lyrical poems; narrative poems; sonnets; shape poems

Informational text provides facts, details, and explanations.

Genre	**Expository text** gives facts about real people, animals, places, and events.	**Persuasive text** tries to convince readers to think or do something.	**Procedural text** tells how to do something in clear, easy-to-understand steps.
Features	The information is factual. It usually includes headings, maps, indexes, time lines, and photos with captions.	Persuasive text tells the author's point of view. There may be persuasive photos or illustrations. There are persuasive words such as *must* and *should*.	The text has a list of necessary materials. There may be maps, diagrams, charts, illustrations, graphs, time lines, or tables.
Organization	The text is often written in sequence. It may start off simply and build to harder information, or the information may be grouped by category.	This is often written with a cause-and-effect or problem-solution pattern. It shows the writer's reasoning in a logical order.	The text is usually chronological. It may be numbered in order of steps.
Includes...	magazine or newspaper articles; essays (cause-and-effect, compare-and-contrast, problem-solution); historical documents	editorials; letters to the editor; advertisements; some speeches; book, movie, or product reviews	instructions or multi-step directions, such as recipes or rules for a game; how-to guides

Literary nonfiction is narrative text based on facts, real events, and real people.

Genre	An **autobiography** is the true story of a real person's life, written by that person. Autobiographical writings include sketches, personal essays, and journals.	A **biography** is the true story of a real person's life, written by another person.
Setting	The setting is a real place from the author's life.	The setting is a real place from the subject's life.
Characters	The characters are real people from real life. An autobiography is written in the first person point of view.	The characters are real people from real life.
Plot	The conflict is often about a great accomplishment or about overcoming a great struggle. It may describe an important event or lesson in the author's life.	The conflict is often about a great accomplishment or about overcoming a great struggle.

I Can Think About...

Fiction

realistic fiction

Is the story one that could really happen?

Is the setting real or a place that seems real?

Do the characters act like real people?

Is the plot realistic and believable?

folk tale

Is there no known author?

Does the story take place "long ago and far away"?

Are the characters portrayed as "good" or "bad"?

What other stories does this remind me of?

legend

Does the story take place in the past?

Are the characters fictional versions of people in history?

Is the main character a hero with superhuman qualities?

historical fiction

Does the story take place in the past?

Is the story focused on a certain time and place in history?

Do characters fit in with a historical time and place?

Do characters overcome a challenge in society?

200

myth

Does the story explain something about nature?

Are the first words "Long ago" or "There once was"?

Can animal characters talk, think, and act like people?

Is there a conflict between a character and nature?

novel

Is this a longer fictional story?

Are the main characters well developed?

Are there side plots and subplots that connect to the main plot?

Can I predict what will happen next based on how characters act?

tall tale

Is the story exaggerated?

Is the story humorous?

Do the characters have superhuman abilities?

Does the story explain why something exists?

I Can Think About...
Nonfiction

biography
Is this the true story of someone's life?
Are the characters real people from real life?
Is there a struggle or accomplishment?

autobiography
Is this the true story of someone's life?
Is this written by the person whose life it is about?
Are the characters real people from real life?
Is there a struggle or accomplishment?

procedural text
Are there numbered steps that tell me what to do?
Is there a list of materials?
Are there diagrams, illustrations, or other graphics?
Is the text a recipe, a set of rules, or other instructions?

persuasive text

Does the text tell the author's point of view?

Are words such as *must* and *should* often used?

Is the text an editorial, an advertisement, or a review?

expository text

Are there facts about real people, animals, places, and events?

Are there maps, time lines, captions, or headings?

Does the text organization have a pattern?

Is this an article or an essay?

I Can Think About...
Drama and Poetry

drama

Is the story meant to be performed?

Is there a description of the setting and a list of characters?

Are there lines of dialogue and stage directions?

Is this a stage play, movie script, skit, or dramatic adaptation?

poetry

Are the words arranged in lines?

Are the lines arranged in stanzas?

Is there rhythm? Is there rhyme?

Are there descriptive words, sound effects, and other poetic elements?

Acknowledgments

Illustrations

7, 9, 11, 13, 15, 17, 19, 21, 23, 25 Ivanke & Lola

Photographs

Every effort has been made to secure permission and provide appropriate credit for photographic material. The publisher deeply regrets any omission and pledges to correct errors called to its attention in subsequent editions.

Unless otherwise acknowledged, all photographs are the property of Pearson Education, Inc.

Photo locators denoted as follows: Top (T), Center (C), Bottom (B), Left (L), Right (R), Background (Bkgd)

33 ©Freelance Photography Guild/Corbis

71 (B) ©Kevin Cooley/Getty Images, (T) ©Michael Krasowitz/Getty Images

81 ©Aurora Photos/Alamy Images

95 (B) ©Shutterstock, (T) ©Olaf Graf/Corbis

99 ©State Museum of Georgia./AKG London Ltd.

101 Pictorial Press Ltd/Alamy

103 ©Underwood & Underwood/Corbis

120 (C) ©ImageState/Alamy Images, (T) ©Michael Gilday/Alamy Images, (B) Jupiter Images

122 (B) ©Christoph von Haussen/Photolibrary Group, Inc., (T) ©Jean JTrome Talbot/Photolibrary, (C) Photolibrary

124 (C) ©Gwendolyn Plath/Getty Images, (B) ©PCL/Alamy Images, (T) Photolibrary

126 (C) ©FB-STUDIO/Alamy Images, (B) ©Jim Naughten/The Image Bank/Getty Images, (T) Corbis

128 (C) ©Imageshop/Corbis, (T) ©Joel Sartore/Photolibrary, (B) Corbis

130 (T) ©Travelshots/Alamy, (C) Alamy, (B) Photolibrary

134 (T) ©Bananastock /Jupiter Images, (B) ©Cut and Deal Ltd/Alamy, (C) ©Kim Karpeles/Alamy Images

138 (T) Laura Doss/Corbis, (B) Flavio Massari/Alamy, (C) Peter Beck/Corbis

139 (BL) Mediscan/Alamy, (BR) Sebastian Kaulitzki/Fotolia

142 (T) Martin Sundberg/Photolibrary/Getty Images, ©Amana productions/Getty Images (B) Kevin O'Hara/Age Fotostock/Alamy

144 (T) Ann Stevens/Alamy, (C) Artur Shevel/Fotolia, (B) Blend Images/Alamy

147 Andrey Kiselev/Fotolia

146 (B) ©Wollwerth Imagery/Fotolia, (T) ©FK PHOTO/Corbis, (C) Photolibrary

148 (B) ©foodfolio/Alamy Images, (T) ©Teresa De Paul/Getty Images, (C) Getty Images

152 (B) ©Heather Angel/Natural Visions/Alamy Images, (C) ©Radius Images /Jupiter Images, (T) ©W. Perry Conway/Corbis

154 (C) ©image100/Corbis, (T) ©Joan Comalat/PhotoLibrary Group, Ltd., (B) Photolibrary

156 (T) ©Michael Brooke/PhotoLibrary Group, Ltd., (B) ©Tom Stoddart/Getty Images, (C) ©WidStock/Alamy

158 (C) ©Aspix/Alamy, (T) ©Frank Greenaway/Getty Images, (B) ©Jason Edwards/National Geographic/Getty Images

159 ©Marty Snyderman/Getty Images

164 (T) ©Ian Edelstein/Alamy Images, (B) ©izmostock/Alamy Images, (C) ©Matthias Kulka/zefa/Corbis

166 (T) ©Dennis Kirkland/Jaynes Gallery/Alamy Images, (C) ©Leonid Ikan/Fotolia, (B) ©Tomas Van Houtryve/Corbis

168 (C) ©allOver photography/Alamy Images, (B) ©Mike Goldwater/Alamy Images, (T) ©TMI/Alamy Images

170 (T) ©David P. Hall/Corbis, (C) ©Randy Faris/Corbis, (B) Getty Images

172 (T) ©Joel Sartore/National Geographic/Getty Images, (C) ©Martin Poole/Getty Images, (B) ©Neil Beckerman/Getty Images

174 (T) ©Barry Austin Photography/Getty Images, (B) ©Monkey Business Images Ltd/Photolibrary, (C) Jupiter Images, World Perspectives/Getty Images

176 (T) Getty Images

177 (B) Bettmann/Corbis

180 (C) ©Monkey Business/Fotolia, (B) ©Robert Kyllo/Shutterstock, (T) ©Misty Bedwell/Design Pics/Corbis

182 (B) ©bst2012/Fotolia, (C) ©Jorgen Larsson/Nordic Photos/Getty Images, (T) ©Randy Faris /Jupiter Images

205